My Near-Death Experience Was Just the Beginning of My Spiritual Journey. . . .

I have seen the hand of God at work in all of our lives. It is in that spirit that I now share some of the journeys I've taken and lessons I've learned in THE AWAKENING HEART.

We have now reached a crossroads, and a Great Awakening has begun in the world. People are hungry for answers and meaning in their lives. We are finally ready for God's message of love, and one of our missions on earth is to grow in the spirit by sharing that love. My prayer is that God will use this book to bring all of us a little closer to completing our missions according to His will.

—Betty J. Eadie, from
THE AWAKENING HEART

Books by Betty J. Eadie

Embraced by the Light
The Awakening Heart: My Continuing Journey to Love*

*Published by POCKET BOOKS

For information regarding special discounts for bulk purchases, please contact Simon & Schuster Special Sales at 1-800-456-6798 or business@simonand schuster.com

The *Awakening Heart*

My continuing journey to love

BETTY J. EADIE

POCKET **STAR** BOOKS

New York   London   Toronto   Sydney

A Pocket Star Book published by
POCKET BOOKS, a division of Simon & Schuster Inc.
1230 Avenue of the Americas, New York, NY 10020

ISBN: 0-671-55878-1

First Pocket Books paperback printing November 1997

10 9 8 7 6 5 4

POCKET STAR BOOKS and colophon are registered
trademarks of Simon & Schuster Inc.

Cover photo of Betty J. Eadie by Judith Ryan
Cover photo of landscape courtesy of Westlight

Printed in the U.S.A.

This book is dedicated:

To my Creator, God. My source of life and
strength, and the giver of love
and all knowledge.

To my family and friends, who stood by me
and made sacrifices as I spent hours
away from them to write.

To my growing number of grandchildren.
They are valiant souls of the next generation.

To the readers of *Embraced by the Light.*
Especially to those who wrote and asked the
questions that inspired this book; I was
encouraged by their prayers and love.

To those in the awakening. May your walk
on this earth lead you straight to the path
of your purpose, and may God's eternal love
continue to be the light that shines
upon you.

Acknowledgments

My eternal love and gratitude to those who contributed intimate details from their lives to share in this book. What they shared was shared with love, and the ripple effect from that will return to them . . . love in its fullest measure.

I especially want to thank my friend and editor Tom Spain. The power of his love and dedication to God first drew me to his spirit. His wisdom and knowledge of editing strengthened me and helped to produce *The Awakening Heart*.

My love and appreciation to Gina Centrello and all the members of Pocket Books, my publisher. What a powerful team of people! Your faith in me and your love for God was evident to me as you did your part in producing this book.

Last, but not least, I am grateful to all who have worked diligently to place *The Awakening Heart* in the bookstores. I think of you as the sowers of love, planting the seed of this book into the furrows created by *Embraced by the Light*.

Contents

Author's Note

*L*ife does not end when we die. Death is a rebirth into a spirit world of light and love, a transition from the physical to the spiritual that is no more frightening or painful than passing between rooms through an open doorway. It is also a joyful homecoming to our natural home, a return to the Creator who sent us here and who welcomes us back with loving arms. I know this, because on November 18, 1973, I experienced death after hemorrhaging from surgery. The events that followed changed my life, and sent me on a journey that continues today.

At the time of my death, I left my body and traveled through a tunnel that stretches between earth and our heavenly home. I was drawn toward a figure of brilliant, radiant light, whom I recognized as my savior, Jesus Christ. I was reunited with loved ones who had passed on before me, and I saw the spirit of my daughter who was yet to be born. I experienced a taste of the life beyond . . . visiting beautiful gardens and the library of knowledge, reliving the Creation and glimpsing the future, watching spirits prepare to come to earth, and witnessing prayers as they were received by angels and answered through the loving care of our Father in heaven.

Most precious of all, I felt the indescribable joy of being embraced by the Savior, who enveloped me with unconditional love and answered the questions I had asked for years. I learned that there are so many religions on earth because we are all at different levels of spiritual development, and that each religion teaches some truth. I saw that there are very few coincidences, and that angels and the spirits of loved ones surround us to help us on earth. I was told that spiritual laws govern our existence, and that each and every part of God's wonderful creation is intimately connected with every other part. I was shown that everything we do has a ripple effect for good or ill on the rest of the world, and I was given a life review before the Council of Men, during which I experienced the effect of all my own thoughts and actions. And I learned that God loves all of us unconditionally, that we are eternal spirits who have come here to grow and learn to love, and that we are received back in heaven with great joy and celebration. The essence of what I learned is that love is supreme, because God is love, and the only way to be like him is to love as he does . . . unconditionally.

I was filled with joy to be in my spiritual home, and I wanted to stay. But I was told that it was not yet my time to die, and that I had a mission to complete on earth before my spirit could return to that place of love again. I understood that each of us has a mission in this life, although we are not allowed to remember what our mission is; after I was shown mine, and my spirit agreed to return to my body to complete it, it was removed from my memory, and I remained unable to remember it after my return to earth.

My near-death experience was just the beginning of my spiritual journey. I understood the importance of sharing my experience and the truths I learned, and I began by describing them in the book *Embraced by the Light*. Since then, my journey has continued with moments of great joy and periods of great challenge. Along the way, my awakening to God has revealed many more remarkable truths, and has led me to people whose trials and triumphs are powerful reminders of why we are here. I have learned much more from my journey, but more than anything else, I have seen the hand of God at work in all of our lives. It is in that spirit that I now share some of the journeys I've taken and lessons I've learned in *The Awakening Heart*.

We have now reached a crossroads, and a Great Awakening has begun in the world. People are hungry for answers and meaning in their lives. We are finally ready for God's message of love, and one of our missions on earth is to grow in the spirit by sharing that love. My prayer is that God will use this book to bring all of us a little closer to completing our missions according to his will.

—Betty J. Eadie
April 1996

The
Awakening
Heart

My Continuing Journey

*N*ight was falling, and I was alone. The room I was sitting in was dark except for a stream of light that poured through the open doorway. I had noticed some furniture and a desk with a telephone on it; other than that I had paid little attention to the rest of the room when I entered a few minutes earlier. The background din of people talking and the squeal of someone adjusting a microphone were reminders that I was in a high school building for a speaking engagement, the last of a two-week series of fifteen presentations.

My book *Embraced by the Light* had been published two weeks earlier, but I had begun speaking about my near-death experience several years before I wrote about it. I already knew that many people were drawn to the message that I shared, because I had seen it change their fear of death and comfort them in their grief. People told me that my experience had given them a greater understanding of God and of his love for them. They, too, shared my joy in the message that I brought back from the Savior: "Above all else, love one another." I could see that the book would help me bring that message to more people than ever before. A new part of my journey was just beginning, and though I wasn't fully awakened to what it would entail, I was excited. After years of struggle, I was living the full, joyful life I had been told we are sent to earth to live, and love was in great abundance.

In sharing my message, I felt the pleasure of fulfilling a purpose, but the constant focus on me and my experience with death was beginning to wear on me. The schedule was very demanding, and I had never spent so much time away from my husband, Joe, and my children. It especially bothered me to be away from little Betty, my youngest daughter, and I was concerned about her reaction to the book's last chapter, which was all about her. She knew she was adopted, but we had never told her the nightmarish details of her earlier life, which I had written about in the final chapter. Now a very secure thirteen-year-old, little Betty was anxious to read *Embraced*, as we referred to it in the family. I had given her a copy just before I left home, and she planned to read it while I was out of town.

As I sat in the darkened room, I had more than homesickness on my mind. I felt a powerful sense of aloneness, a feeling that had swept over me often in the years since my return. In the past two weeks it had been stronger than ever before, and somehow different, reaching to the depths of me. At times it would blanket my entire spirit without warning, causing me to weep. I didn't understand these emotions, though I guessed they were connected with the responsibility I felt for the message I was sharing. But I sensed there was more. I knew that I had returned from my experience to complete a mission, though I did not know what it was or if the work I was now doing was part of it. Even as I had entered the building tonight, I felt terribly alone, in purpose and in responsibility.

"Betty . . . ?" Curtis Taylor, one of my publishers, called my name as he joined me. "Oh, there you are. Are you ready? It's a full house." There was a lot of excitement in his voice . . . until he sensed that something was troubling me.

"Betty," he spoke again, "you're frightened. Don't be!"

Frightened? Oddly enough, I had not felt that emotion in years. I had known my share of fear, but God had shown me the way to overcome fear years ago. During the past two weeks, I felt strengthened by exceptional feelings of confidence, serenity, and peace each time I shared my story. I also experienced an indescribable energy that ran through me like currents of electricity, energizing my body, every nerve, fiber, and cell. Sometimes I felt as if I would burst if I did not find a way to diffuse it.

"No . . . I'm not frightened," I thought. "I'd probably feel more human if I were." I asked Curtis to pray with me, my voice catching, though I tried to hold it back. As we prayed, I began to sense a multitude of angels also in attendance there. This night was going to be different. I could always tell by the power of resistance. A soul, perhaps even more than one, would benefit from tonight's experience.

I thought of the beautiful power of the ripple effect that I had been shown, and I knew that reaching even just one soul with the message of God's love would set in motion a reaction that passed that hopeful message to others and then more, rippling out to reach countless souls. It was already in motion by the time we had all arrived tonight; the ripple effect had brought me to this school as well as everyone else who was here with me. But my heart was still feeling heavy and burdened as I heard the familiar introduction begin.

My thoughts drifted back to the reason I had written *Embraced*. At the time, I had not wanted to write it. So many years had passed since my experience, and so much had happened. I was where I wanted to be professionally and had worked hard to get there. My husband, Joe, and I had worked hard to build a nest egg, too, and it was time to enjoy it. No, I hadn't wanted to give up everything I had worked so hard for. But when the call came to write it, I knew that I would. God had made it clear that he wanted his message sent through me, and I had long ago learned to answer God's call when it came.

Suddenly reminded once again of where I was, I heard the introduction come to its close, ". . . and I want you to meet the most honest woman that I know, Betty Jean Eadie."

As the curtains parted once again, my cue to step forward, I could feel the love in the room that we all shared, the love that had brought us all here and that we all wanted to know more about. Still, I could not help but think of the pain that I hid and the faith that led me through my long spiritual struggle. Love, faith, and struggle . . . all of these were in my thoughts as I took a deep breath and stepped out into the bright lights. I knew that after this night I would never be the same again.

I shared my experience, feeling all of the pain and joy, and all of the sorrow, as though it had happened only days before. I had never doubted the validity of what happened to me. But I have questioned my worthiness for being chosen to have the experience. I knew, from what I was told in the spirit world, that nothing is by chance. I was also told that all things, both positive and negative, provided opportunities for growth and that they were often placed in our lives for a purpose. I knew that my journey to the spirit world and back did not occur by happenstance. But I did not know why it happened to me. *Why ME, God? Why?* I prayed for an answer often, but no answer came.

For years, I had asked God that question in solitude. No one else had ever demanded to know the answer, and only I knew that I could not provide it. But tonight, as I stood before the audience, the question came. "Betty, why do you think that you were chosen for this awesome experience?" asked a man in the audience. "Could you please explain, Why You?" There was a note of sarcasm in the man's voice as he continued his questioning. "Wouldn't God have chosen a member of the clergy or the priesthood to come back with the information that you say you have been given?"

A part of me felt instantly defensive, "Why NOT me?" I was ready to respond out of frustration. But instead of enjoying the sweetness of retaliation, I remained silent. The painful fact was, I didn't know the answer. I felt that the audience had the right to ask me, as I had God, and I still needed to know the answer for myself. But who was responsible for the answer . . . God or me?

I knew that returning to my body had not been a conscious decision or a mortal choice. The knowledge and unconditional love that I experienced in the spirit world were so beautiful that no spiritual being could possibly desire to leave unless it was for a higher purpose, although I could not recall the mission that brought me back from that place of light and love. My spirit had made that decision based upon information that had permeated my higher conscious being, the place in me where pure knowledge and unconditional love is connected to God. My soul yearned to go back there from the moment that I realized I had returned to my body.

Joe had stayed with me that morning, nineteen years ago, for as long as he could before going back home to be with our children. He held my hand as I drifted in and out of what appeared as sleep to him. But while my body remained in the bed, my spirit bridged a gap between two worlds—one, this earthly plane, and the other, a place that remains indescribably wonderful and full of mysteries.

As I lay on the hospital bed still unable to move, I was shown scenes of what would become of the earth and of us who occupied it. The heavenly beings continuously taught me through visual images, much like a slide show, with specific parts activated to emphasize important things for me to remember. I watched captivated, but felt as though I was experiencing the events as they happened.

I was shown that the earth, too, had a spirit life, an

energy that God gave it so that it could produce life-giving substances for our benefit. Then, as its inhabitants, we lent our own energy to that energy, changing the earth's to match our own. I saw that the atmosphere surrounding our earth was saturated with combustible components that had threatened our lives for years and were now ready to do further destruction. I knew that this was the effect of our greed and other sins we had committed against the earth, and we would have to suffer the consequences of that.

As I continued to observe, I saw our mountains, the majestic peaks that once stood solid and firm, burst into runny streams of molten rocks that smoothed out like melted chocolate. A shimmer of deep water glistened on land that was once desert, and a dark brown fog covered all else that I could see. People wandered aimlessly. They, too, appeared to be in darkness. Little life was left in them and great sorrow filled their hearts.

"This world belongs to you, Father," my spirit wept. "It was placed in our care. . . . Now we have destroyed it!"

I continued to watch scene after scene in amazement, like an observer at a fatal accident. So this is our creation, I thought. I knew that this was never God's will for our lives! He created us like himself and gave us gifts, special talents to develop and to use as we chose. He is the pattern that we are to follow, and his example would be the greatest respect to the earth that so richly gives of all it has. I thought back to the Savior's final words to me: "The days of the earth are short." I wondered if there was anything we could do before we met with this devastation.

After I was given this vision, I was told that I would recall specific knowledge as I needed it or would receive it by way of visions or visitations. My entire journey was capsulated, and additional information that I knew I would be using later on was superimposed. This information was then stored in my subconscious mind with specific dates and times for its release. I knew I could choose to access this information sooner, if I so desired, but I understood it was God's will for me to follow his timing. My visitations in the spirit world grew shorter that morning, but I longed to remain where I had been.

My doctor's presence brought me to physical awareness again when he leaned over me and asked "Betty, it's been a tough night, how do you feel?" I wanted to tell him to go away, but the concern in his eyes softened my reply. "I'm okay, I guess, thanks," I answered. "Do you want to talk about it," he continued, and reaching for my hand, he patted it gently. I felt that what I had just experienced was too sacred, too awesome, to put into words at this moment. "I've had a nightmare, I guess, but I'm really okay now," I heard myself explain. I wanted to just be left alone to think and to continue to experience the other side. I closed my eyes and turned my face away, still wanting to tell him to go away and wondering if I'd made the wrong decision by coming back here. Just let go, Betty, and go back, THERE! I thought. They had told me not to focus on the reason for my return, that it would come later, but I couldn't help but wonder what the reason could be. I felt uncomfortable not knowing; what could I have promised to do that was so important? For God . . . for me?

"I see you are very tired," I heard my doctor saying. His voice was more of a whisper now, and I knew he was exhausted from having been up with me most of the night. He asked a nurse to give me something so that I could rest better. Then, I felt a needle penetrate the skin of my forearm and its contents spread through my body, closing out the thoughts that would live with me for the rest of my life. "What did I promise to do, God, what is my mission, and why me?"

Why me? Almost two decades later, the question hung in the air like a weighted drape. I stood silent on the stage unable for a moment to answer. I knew that my whole life had brought me to this point, as I had known for years that I would do whatever it took to do the will of my Heavenly Father, so that I could return to him and to my *natural* home. Completing my mission was what God had wanted me to do . . . he had prepared me to do it. After my experience, he stripped me of my old perceptions, so that I could use all of my talents to share the message he had given me. It had not been easy. My life since my return from the spirit world had been a difficult journey of awakening, a journey that I knew would continue to unfold in years ahead. I had not brought myself here: I had only followed. And though at times I feel profoundly alone on my journey, I know that he is leading others, too, and that our sharing of his message of love is part of his plan.

I leaned into the microphone and heard myself whisper, "I don't know the answer. . . . I wish I did, though." It was the only answer I could give . . . the answer from my heart. And as I said the words that finally gave voice to the aloneness I had felt for so long, my heart opened to the full mystery and wonder of the journey that had brought me here, and to the journey that still lay ahead. I thought of the visions I had been given as I returned to my body, and I knew that I had much further to go before I would return to my spiritual home. I saw that my service was only beginning and that there would be many more nights like this one . . . countless more chances to share the hope, joy, and comfort that can only be found in the love of God.

My mission was not over. My journey, I saw now, was my life. I could not know of the joys that it would bring me, but I knew that I was on the path God wanted, and that was all I needed to know. For all of us who listen, in the stillness of our hearts, God enlightens us and offers to lead the way.

My Recovery

My memories of the spirit world were a source of comfort and inspiration during the difficult transition back to my life in my body. As the week of recovery in the hospital passed, family and friends visited, but my mind could focus only on what I could not talk about. I wanted to share my experience with them, but the right words would not come. Back as a mortal being, I had only the English language to express thoughts and events that *no* earthly language was capable of communicating. Frustrated, I gave up trying to verbalize them, and I seldom brought the subject up again. Joe didn't question me or ask for further details, and I could tell that he actually became uncomfortable at the mention of my experience.

On several occasions, I noticed him thoughtfully watching me, often with tears in his eyes, and I knew that what preoccupied and frightened him most was that he had almost lost me!

I was more interested in reliving the experience in my mind than discussing it. I would vividly recall each moment spent with Jesus in detail—not trying to hold on to the memory for fear of losing it, but rather thrilling each time to my newfound love for God and the freedom I received from it. I remembered his incredible countenance, and how powerfully it reminded me that, other than God, my eternal Father, none other was greater than he. He was Jesus, my Lord and Savior, and yet I knew that what we named him was unimportant to him. I knew that he had the ability to appear to me or others in more than one way . . . however it was necessary for us to experience him and accept him. As I had looked at Jesus in all his glory, somehow I knew that not only was I accepting of his presence, but I was worthy of him. Jesus, I "knew," need never show me the nail prints in his hands nor the gash in his side as proof of who he was. I belonged to him just as I was, and the fact that he had suffered pain was not the issue now. His divine expression of love was, and I never questioned that.

The aura surrounding his body was brilliant white and full of energy. Although this light shone brightly around him, I saw that he *was* the light and it came from within him. Light reflected off what appeared to me to be his flesh. His crystalline body resembled what could be spun light, though it was solid and firm, having the three dimensions of length, breadth, and thickness. Prisms of intense light spiraled, pulsated, and moved with each minuscule change in his thoughts or desires. His eyes, though liquid with his love, somehow danced like fire, flickering with energy and life when he needed to express to me his most sincere and earnest wishes for me. I have sought out many pictures of Jesus since my return, and some capture an emotion that I saw him express, but an exact portrait of him in all his glory would be impossible to paint with the materials and colors we have here on earth.

Our communication was nonverbal, all thoughts and feelings that we chose to express were expressed directly, straight from his heart to mine and vice versa. Still, our communication could be felt and understood by others when it was meant to be. Our nonverbal exchange was translated to our language here and impressed firmly into me as I would understand it as a mortal being. The language expressed there could certainly be described as universal in nature. I understood perfectly every word that Jesus "spoke" to me, to the council of men, and to my spiritual guides. Sometimes I would actually feel and experience his voice. When this happened, it was meant to be more personal, in that his voice resonated within me, the rich vibrant tones actually penetrating my spiritual being. It came as a melody that I could feel as if I were an instrument he was playing. His voice gave me life, and I became healed by it. No greater joy have I experienced since his unconditional love for me!

The rays of light surrounding Jesus were filled with knowledge and love. Just standing in his presence and absorbing it gave me the ability to expand the love and knowledge within. My spiritual body filled to almost bursting with his divine love and understanding. I became a part of all there ever was, living it, experiencing it, then somehow nurtured by it. The spirit, not unlike the human mind, must be *receptive* and *flexible* in order to expand and develop as I did. I never thought that I had either of these qualities, but I could accept the fact that all things are possible through God.

I had thought that I looked forward to returning to my home and family, but when I entered the front door, everything seemed strange and uninviting. I felt closed in. Trapped. My spirit recalled another place more comforting and pleasant. I needed the space, color, and melodies that had filled me with healing, loving tones. That beautiful place had also been filled with people whom I loved dearly; while I could no longer recall a name or face, nevertheless, I knew I had loved them deeply, and my heart yearned for them now.

Coming back from the spirit world gave me a new awareness of this world. It changed not only the way I saw the world, but the way I saw myself. The things that I had once desired for my family and for myself were no longer so appealing. I used to long for material things, and I had sacrificed for many of them. But now I could see how easy it is to get caught up in materialism—and how it can hold *us* back from *our* spiritual focus! I had let my interests get caught up with things, and then those things began to own me!

I still wanted to have nice things, but my greater desire was that my heart not be possessed by them, not wrapped up in them. I had kept my bedroom off limits to my children. With six little ones around the house, it had not only been the cleanest room in the house, but a room where I could keep my little treasures without fear of the kids breaking them. The children would stand in the doorway as if it were roped off, gazing into the forbidden room.

I no longer felt the need to keep the children away. Instead, I gathered them into my room, where we would sit and talk for hours . . . all six of them and me, on my bed! No longer the forbidden room, it became a family sanctuary for openness and sharing. We came to love our new closeness, and I developed a new appreciation for my family. My ego had played the larger part in the way I had raised them prior to my near-death experience. Now I needed to undo the damage I had done. I had learned during my experience that my children were previously developed spiritual beings like myself. We were friends before this earth life, and we wanted to remain together for this life's lessons and experiences. We had bonded as soul friends there and chose to come here as a family, sharing our experiences with each other to further our spiritual development. I knew that as parents, Joe and I could most honor that bond by giving them the best of us while they were young and guiding them by example, setting a standard by which they could grow strong. By allowing them space within our guidance, to make their own mistakes, we would be acting out our Heavenly Father's plan of free will used toward spiritual growth. When our children became adults, Joe and I would need only to stand by them and give them strength when they needed it, rather than to express our own egos by interfering in their lives and dominating them. They, too, had an obligation to us, their parents, and to each other for the rest of their lives.

I began to see that I had given my family many misconceptions about God and about life in general and that they would extend this knowledge to their families and then to society. We are like empty vessels when born: whatever fills us then, is what we later pour. I had taught my children what I had learned about God, warning them time after time that God watches over them and knows all their "sins." They came to think as I had, that if they did the least thing wrong, something bad would happen to them and that God would be responsible for it! My fears were being expressed in them. I had not meant to use this in a threatening, punishing way, but as a warning—just as I had received. But because of this, my children carried with them fear and guilt that impeded their development and love for God.

My entire outlook on God was changed now, and I began to teach my children differently. First I taught them that God loved them unconditionally and that they were a part of him—literally, his spiritual children. As a parent he wanted only the best for them and would give that to them if their hearts so desired it. We prayed differently, too, from our hearts, not just from our lips in repetition as I had taught them before. They also needed to know that God does not punish them by making bad things happen in their lives, but that these things often happened because of the cause and effect of our wrong decisions or the decisions of others.

These were among the thoughts that occupied me as I reviewed my experience and reflected on things that no other person in my life could understand. I enjoyed solitude and silence in my room, and although I no longer made it off limits to others, at times I sought its privacy to be alone with my thoughts.

The off-white walls of my bedroom that once appeared fresh and pleasing to me now lacked life and energy. I wanted color—bright, radiant color—to surround me like the garden in the spirit world. As soon as I was well enough to shop for paint, I chose the color magenta for my bedroom and painted all four walls the same. The richness of color filled my spirit with joy and brought back feelings of wholesomeness and life as I remembered it from experience. I painted the bathroom rose and white and the kitchen a yellow-green that reminded me of new growth on a tree in spring. I had learned that this shade of green was a healing color, and the kitchen seemed the appropriate place for it.

My frenzy for color didn't seem to bother anyone, until I painted the living room a vibrant orange! That morning I had been by myself when I finished my breakfast juice and placed the glass on a braided straw coaster. One of the braids caught my eye. It was dyed orange-red, and I could not take my eyes off it. The energy in that particular color lifted my spirits to a new high. I immediately took the coaster to the paint store, and they were able to make an exact match. I started painting as soon as I returned home, and in just a few short hours all the walls in the front room were brightly illuminated. The late afternoon sun shone through the large bay windows, creating a magnificent effect. As I sat in a chair and stared at the color, my spirit felt vibrantly alive for the first time since my return—that is, until Joe walked in and I caught the look on his face.

"I guess I carried things too far?" I stammered.

"I can't believe you these days," he spoke softly, still in shock. "I don't know each night who or what I'm coming home to. The neighbors stopped me as I drove up; one of them was going to call the fire department when he caught a glimpse of the walls through the windows. Seriously, Betty, haven't you have gone a bit too far with this?"

I realized I had been considering my own comfort, not Joe's or the rest of the family's. I needed so very much for him to understand me . . . and yet, how could he? "Honey, I have to have color and light! I yearn for it! But we can paint it back to white," I apologized.

Joe wrapped his arms around me and held me tight. "Sweetheart, I'll learn to live with it if that is what you want. Making you happy is all that has ever been important to me; I just want you back as you were before. If this pleases you, let's leave it as it is." I knew that he was trying hard to understand my sudden change, my new needs. I had prayed that God would help us both to make the appropriate adjustments while I achieved some balance in my life.

Together we replaced all the furniture and pictures. The walls in the front room have been painted many times since then, but the color remained that vibrant orange until we moved from that house twenty years later.

Adjustments between my spiritual and natural self continued. It wasn't easy for me to live in two worlds, the spiritual world and this one. They often conflicted—sometimes because of the way I wanted things to be, but more often because of the ideas and attitudes that were imposed on me. My response to life had changed, too. I more readily and openly accepted people, forgave and loved them in a deeper way—more unconditionally. I found that this type of love often threatened those who did not understand it. They would become uncomfortable and begin looking for ulterior motives.

Television bothered me the most, perhaps because it could instantly intrude in my home. I had watched the daytime serials, unable to miss a single day; I was addicted to them. Now I never watched them. They felt like a personal attack on my spirit, and it pained me to think of those who lived each day of their lives, as I had, saturated in what was being expressed here as normal. I knew that our spirits could mutate over time, acquiring layers and layers of mortal desires until they destroyed the sweetness of the spirit and we accepted them as a natural and acceptable part of our being.

My sudden change in attitude was difficult for my family at first. The children now had to get my approval before watching any television or going to the movies with friends. Even some of what Joe watched, which had previously been perfectly acceptable, grated on me spiritually. I began to prefer spending more of my evenings alone in my room while the family watched many of the old familiar programs that had once excited me.

Material things, though often necessary, seemed temporary and artificial to my spirit. I cared little for the things of the earth now; they no longer held my interest.

Instead I was powerfully and undeniably drawn to anything that reminded me of the wonders I had seen and experienced. I knew that greater, indescribable things existed, and that in comparison, what we developed here on earth resembled the drawings and creations of my little children.

All of my interests had changed, and I was painfully aware that my life before had been very shallow. I had a new interest now, an unquenchable thirst for greater spiritual knowledge, but I didn't know where to find it. Old friends stopped coming by; the things we had shared before—gossip sessions, parties, shopping, and, of course, the afternoon soaps—no longer held any interest for me. I had never felt more alone in my entire life.

Joe's work began to require he spend more of his time away from home, and with our growing financial needs, we were happy for the overtime. But the long periods of time alone made me begin to turn inward with emotions I could not share nor understand. Each morning I awoke, my thoughts were the same. I was homesick for a place that did not exist here on earth, a place that my heart longed for. The sounds and melodies of that heavenly garden where everything glorified God was not reproducible on earth. And I desired more than anything else some small amount of the love that I experienced there, but found that nothing here compared. I now understood why it was important for us to go through the "veil of forgetting" when we come to earth . . .

because remembering is so horrifically painful. I so missed the warmth of God's eternal, unconditional love. To be without it is the way I imagined hell would be.

In the past, it had been easy for me to make any adjustments necessary to survive. I had often done so without thought. But now, the adjustments were not coming to me, and I began to feel that any hope for the survival of my soul was dwindling rapidly. I didn't know what to do with the knowledge I had been given; it seemed more to have been imposed on me than taught to me. I felt lost and alone. Joe had tried to comfort me by listening with patience and care, but he could only comprehend the external changes in me, not the deeper spiritual feelings that I needed to express. I began to feel rejected and abandoned by God.

In my agony I turned to God in prayer, and I found that I could express myself to him. Prayer became my only solace and the life preserver that I clung to. While in the presence of God, I had understood that knowledge and belief precede faith. When we learn of God and believe in him, we acquire faith in him. When we experience that faith, it develops further. I knew I had to use the faith I had acquired, but I did not know where to begin.

I thought about what I had learned and believed already. I knew that God hears *all* prayers and answers them in their right time, according to his plan for each of us. I knew that as part of his plan—as part of our growth—God may allow us to go through trials in a sorting-out period, a cleansing, a purification time when we are often forced to make new decisions based upon our *current* faith and trust in him. Each of us develops like a diamond in the rough. The jagged edges are then chipped away and unnecessary roughness removed until we are multifaceted, with many points of view, all the while growing less judgmental and more compassionate from having experienced the pain of living.

I saw that I could trust in prayer. I knew and believed that if I asked for God's will to be done in my life, my prayers would be answered in their time. I began to exercise my faith by prayer, as I had learned, thanking God for all things, no matter how negative they first appeared. I could now see that God was teaching me *how* to be patient and wait on him. Trusting him, believing in him, and knowing that he really is in control, I knew he will give us, his beloved children, the righteous desires of our hearts when we ask for them. I asked for his help and guidance to endure my most difficult moments and future trials to the end.

I soon learned I was not yet prepared for the challenges ahead.

The Gift to Heal

As the months passed after my return from the hospital, I began to notice that I felt different. Outwardly I appeared the same to my family, but I had changed. I felt I had lost the basis for my future as a mother, wife, and individual because I "knew"—I had been shown— that my children and husband could live out their lives perfectly well without me. I knew from my experience that I had a purpose, a mission, but it was beyond the recall of my conscious mind, and I simply felt I had no reason to continue to live on earth. Unhappy and dissatisfied with every aspect of my life, I regretted that I had agreed to come back, and I sank deeper and deeper into despair.

Then one morning I awoke to silence. I could feel the vibration of sound . . . but not the sound itself. I used to listen to my children's feet as they ran up and down the stairs every morning, and I would remind them not to run. But this morning was different: as I lay in bed, my left ear on the pillow, I just felt them running on the stairs. Hundreds of tests followed over the next couple of years with no explanation of how I had lost the hearing in my right ear, but the diagnosis was deafness due to nerve damage to the inner ear. Suddenly, I could not tell the direction from which any sound came. Everything became a new challenge, and I quickly learned to rely upon my other senses for help in almost everything I did.

While losing my hearing posed some physical difficulties for me, my spirit was strangely unaffected. When the doctor first told me that I would never hear in that ear again, I remember saying, "I'm thankful to God that I have two ears." I could not explain to the doctor that my spirit was not offended by the loss of something physical. I was, however, becoming aware of the reason I was suffering emotionally: my spirit was offended by its return to the physical and by my spiritual loss. I wanted to go home, to the beautiful natural home that I knew we all came from, and my heart was filled with grief.

The spiritual offense soon began to manifest itself in my body; I became physically tired and weak. Days would pass when even bathing became a chore. My appearance no longer meant anything to me; I seldom wore makeup or paid attention to how I dressed. For the first time in my life I gained a tremendous amount of weight and refused to be included in family photographs. Slowly, I lost interest in my home and its upkeep. I was so mentally depressed that I even canceled doctor appointments, feeling too ill to go. I changed doctors often, hoping to find one with the right answers to my dilemma, and though they treated me with medicines of all kinds, nothing helped.

When I saw that my depression was also affecting my family, I again sought help from God, renewing my commitment to prayer. I remembered the power I had seen in prayers as they were sent up to God, and I tried to visualize energy into my prayers. But I didn't have the strength to do even that. I had little energy left in me to fight back. God had deserted me, it seemed, and I could not understand why!

As more months passed with no improvement, I withdrew further into myself. I desperately needed someone with whom I could share my experience, someone who had spiritual knowledge of God. The experience was more alive to me than anything that I had ever known before; in comparison, "that" was reality, and this was death. I was more than homesick. My spirit felt painfully misplaced. My desire to be with God created such a vacuum in my life that I prayed that I would be taken home soon. I taped an account of my near-death experience just in case my prayers were answered; I wanted Joe and my children to know that I would be truly happy after I left this earth. I also wanted them to know that I could check on them from time to time and though I loved them and they me, they would be fine without me. I had no desire to take my own life, nor could I have done that, but when death did not come, though I fought further despair, I became less able to cope with my life.

Then, one morning, I had my first anxiety attack. I was on the phone talking to a friend when my heart started pounding wildly and suddenly I couldn't breathe. I thought I was having a heart attack, so I hurried off the phone. That attack passed, but more followed, and the visits to the doctors began again. With each frightening attack, my way of life changed a little more, as the list of locations and activities I associated with the panic grew. Soon, I had few "safe" places, and the fear that I had developed became my worst enemy.

My battle with fear kept me from seeking spiritual guidance outside my home. I prayed and read the Bible when I could concentrate, but that was not often, nor was it for long. I fought for control, to keep the external signs of my internal struggle from my family. I didn't want to burden anyone else and was ashamed that I could not handle what was happening to me. But my fears disabled me still further. I became agoraphobic.

Fear is contagious and rapidly spreads to all who are exposed to it. Without their knowing it, my family and friends fed my fears daily with their concern for me. I was not encouraged to handle things on my own, and I often overheard them telling each other, "You know she shouldn't be alone." They drove me everywhere, staying with me in lines at the stores or even shopping for me. Though I was grateful for their help—I could not have lived without their support—I saw how my fears limited everyone around me, our interactions so interdependent that it was hard to determine who had the fear.

I learned from my struggle that illness or wellness is the responsibility of each individual, a burden that should not be shared for long periods of time. I hid many of my fears from Joe and my family, but I knew that they sensed them anyway. I spent most of my time in the safety of my bedroom and kitchen when they were away at work and school, and I continued my prayers to God, despite the feeling that I received no answers.

Help finally came the day I was led to open my Bible to four specific verses. The first was Proverbs 16:3: "Commit thy work unto the Lord, and thy thoughts shall be established." During my experience, I had learned that our thoughts create our lives. Knowing this, I had tried to change my thoughts, but that had not worked. I could not concentrate long enough to do it.

I was then led to Matthew 6:33: "But seek ye first the kingdom of God and his righteousness and all these things shall be added unto you." I had also been shown that the kingdom of God was *within* us, that we are the temple of God and he dwells there when we let him. I had also witnessed that God is love, and I knew that without love in my heart—not just for others, but for myself—I was lost. I no longer loved my mortal self; I had seen my spiritual being. This body was like clay, heavy, cumbersome, and abhorrent to me.

The final two verses were Matthew 7:7–8: "Ask, and it shall be given you: seek and ye shall find: knock and it shall be opened unto you. For everyone that asketh receiveth: and he that seeketh findeth; and to him that knocketh it shall be opened."

These verses confirmed what I already knew, what I had *seen*, but now I understood that in my misery I had lost my faith in God. I remembered I had been told knowledge comes before faith, and while it was clear that I had knowledge of his existence, had even experienced his presence, I realized now that I had not *internalized* it, made it a part of me.

Ask? I had done that, but I hadn't been focused enough to know what to ask for. And though I had asked for help, I had not been open to receive it until I let go of my ego and allowed God to guide me to the answers, as he did now. I had been blind before, shielding my eyes from everything except me and my self-pity.

Ask. Seek. Knock. These are action words of faith. But before any of these could be applied, I had to have desire as my driving force. I had that now, and I knew that my continued journey would require a powerful faith, in God, in me, and in the world that surrounds me.

I thought of the laws of healing that were taught to me in the spirit world. I had learned each of us is responsible for our body while on earth, that it is up to us to tap into the power within us that affects the health of our body, mind, and spirit and important to bring the three into harmony. I knew that spiritual healing must precede physical and mental healing and that we determine whether our spirits draw on the positive or the negative energy available to us. I had been shown that the self-centeredness of depression can create further illness and that the cycles of fear and guilt that draw one into darkness are Satan's greatest tools.

I began to see now, for the first time, many of my own weaknesses and recognized that I had the ability to overcome my own creations. I also knew I could deny other illnesses the power to express themselves in me. I had learned that one of the greatest skills we can acquire is the ability to let go. To achieve the balance we need, we must let go of the congestive forces in our lives, everything that is weighty or burdensome on our spirits. But I had been holding on to the spirit world that I had left . . . I wanted to continue to bathe in the love of Christ. I believed that I could not live in a world that was full of fear, the world in which I currently lived. Now I saw that I was so involved in what I had once experienced that not only was I out of balance, I was breaking a fundamental law of health. I was trapped in spiritual gluttony.

I was shown that gluttony is a sin and that it can

involve more than just food. Gluttony of anything, including our dwelling on the past and the mistakes we made there, can enslave us. The *would have*'s, *should have*'s, and *could have*'s are all ties to the past, and they can bind us unless we let them go. I saw that I was enslaved and unable to move forward. I was not where I needed to be . . . in the present. I needed to let go of the past by creating love here and now, in my life and in the world I now lived in. I vowed to change my sick spirit by doing service, having faith, and sharing love, the acts that I had been shown are among the reasons God placed us here.

I began to heal. At first I started doing small things—fixing a meal for sick friends, baby-sitting for young parents who needed time to be alone together, making calls to older people who were shut in. These first small steps led to more, and then still more. I continued doing service because it required my energy and focus, and I enjoyed the love that I received in return.

I studied the use of herbs and vitamins and began to use them to strengthen my body. I first exercised by walking to the end of the block, making the entire block my goal by the end of the month. Soon I could walk around the block by myself without anxiety and set another goal of a mile, five blocks out and five back. I timed myself, so when I became frightened, I would look at my watch and remind myself that in so many minutes I would be "safe" again at home, and I challenged myself to be brave enough to continue until then. Each time out

I became more confident, and with each step I told myself that I would rather die on my feet than sitting at home in my bedroom. It took some time, but sooner than I had imagined, I was walking six miles each day, stopping at nearby parks to feed the ducks as they swam in the ponds. The daily panic attacks abated as I learned to deal with them, and the agoraphobia became less of a problem as I ventured out. I still had boundaries, but they were expanding.

When I became proficient with herbs, I used them to treat minor ailments of my children, and they seldom got sick anymore. Joe watched me curiously but did not want any treatment for his own illnesses until he got an infection from a cut on his foot. In spite of antibiotics that the doctor prescribed, the infection spread, and soon Joe's entire foot, from his ankle down, turned red and was swollen. Gangrene had settled into his toe and was moving up his foot; the doctor told us he might have to remove Joe's foot if antibiotics didn't help. When they didn't help, I convinced Joe to let me try herbs. I immediately went to work gathering the herbs that I needed. I combined a mixture of herbs into a poultice I placed on Joe's foot, changing the dressing every hour throughout the night. Each time I changed the poultice, I marked with a pen the outline of the red swollen area on his foot. By morning we counted each circle where the swelling had been; there was no redness or swelling to be seen, and Joe's foot was saved. The doctor was amazed, but was not surprised at what I had used, having some familiarity with herbal medicine himself.

Using herbs had come naturally to me. I had studied some, but I felt that the use of herbs and their combination was more of a gift, as if I were tapping into some knowledge I didn't know I had. As I continued developing my talents, both temporal and spiritual, I learned that my cell memory was beginning to awaken to knowledge stored there through my ancestry . . . my Native American gift to heal.

As I continued the process of opening up to God and letting go, I healed more rapidly. My service to others led me to new friends, and I was blessed by their love. More important, God could reach me because of my open heart, and I began to experience again his loving presence in great abundance. The first of those moments happened when I awakened from an afternoon nap to see lights of brilliant colors moving around me. There was no sound—a stillness instead. I sensed that the room was full of lights, many lights. I sat up and watched them as they danced around me. I felt an energy from them that filled me with love. They left after just a few moments, but a couple of weeks later they visited again.

This time I had not been sleeping but was standing outside where I usually stood to pray, and I heard them before I saw them. They were filled with song and music that I recognized from the spirit world. Joe walked out just in time to hear the very end of their song. He stood disbelieving as I whispered to him what it was that he was hearing. He heard what he heard, and though he could not make sense of it, he knew that he had experienced something wonderful. Each time they came I experienced them a little differently, but I knew that I was in the presence of angels who had sung to me just before I returned to earth. With song, light, and brilliant color, they continued to express to me that whatever the struggles I was facing, I was in the right place. I was surrounded with God's love, and all was well.

Seeking the Presence of God

The search for God's presence in my life was more important now than ever before. I was compelled first to find him in everything that surrounded me, then to seek his presence within me. When I began to see him unexpectedly, everywhere, in everyone and everything, my soul delighted, and I felt as a child would feel, seeing everything for the first time and from a clearer perspective. My rebirth into this world had at first brought me fear of this distant place, far from my original home; now I began to see its beauty. I awoke each morning to feelings of expectation, excited that God had given me another day to experience life. I knew that I was learning to use my God-given free will to become a creator like him. By granting us free will, as I had been shown, God gave us the privilege to express ourselves and to accept the responsibility of choice—or the burden of choice, depending upon what our motivations were.

God began to prepare me for the windows of opportunity to exercise my will, and while I knew those same windows could come around more than once, I knew, too, that I had to stay in tune with him to recognize the golden opportunity the first time it came around, the golden moment when the window was open. I knew that if I was not ready the first time it appeared, a second time was possible, but if it came around again, I would have to open it myself.

The more difficult part of my search for God's presence was to find him in me, so that I would be ready to serve him on a moment's notice if need be. Every now and then, I got a clear image of him in me and what he wanted for me, but the image would fade quickly; I was having difficulty maintaining a Christ-like spirit in the world.

Once I was crossing the street with one of my younger children when a young woman drove up in a car, slowing down as we entered the crosswalk. Apparently changing her mind, she suddenly sped up, coming close to hitting my child in front of me. She frightened both herself and us, but instead of an apology, she swore obscenities at my child for being in her way. Acting on old schoolyard instinct, I reached through the open window of the car and slapped her mouth. This surprised both of us, as I had thought that I would not behave in such a way after my experience.

At times like this, I knew that I was not yet living God's will. God is love, in its purest form. His love seeks nothing from us and demands nothing of us. His love is unconditionally given to all who believe in him. To be in his presence and share his love, we must become as he is and learn to love without judgments and conditions. I had not found it easy to love or to be loved before. Love requires an ability to trust, but I had been hurt before by love. I was separated from my family and their love as a child. I was told I was loved at the boarding schools I was sent to, but I was just as often punished and hurt, often in the name of God.

My first marriage fell apart even though I had loved. Love to me was always conditional, based on the requirements of those who received my love and conditioned by whatever motivated them or me at that time. I understood the fullness of love now that I had experienced it with Jesus, and I desired it now, here on earth, with all my heart—not only in my life, but within me as I had felt it before.

I reflected on the unconditional love, and the pure knowledge of love, that I experienced in the spirit realm. I remembered that the light that radiated from Jesus was knowledge filled with love, while the dimmer light I had noticed in me was more of a desire for love than love itself. The longer I remained in his presence, however, the brighter my light glowed, absorbing some of his light, which he shared with me. Then, just before my return, I noticed that my spirit also emanated an abundance of light—light that was full to overflowing with love! It was his presence of love that I had absorbed, and it expanded me. I knew that as mortals we are to share light and love with each other, blending with and expanding each other—a spiritual exchange of energy, not the selfish pursuit of physical love. Like attracts like. Just as fear is contagious, so is love. My desire to love and be loved was evident in my countenance.

I did not know how to express such love after my return, but I knew that I had the desire to learn. Love would come to me because I was receptive, open, and tender, and that was all that was necessary. God "knew" my heart. His love for me found no barrier, and my love for him would never end.

I once heard that "you find love when you give it away." That made sense to me because that was exactly what happened to me in my embrace with the Lord. He gave me love, and I returned it, not knowing that I had love to give. So I began to practice giving love, at first sending it out by thought to people whom I wanted to love, then actually expressing it to them. Soon the art of loving became one my greatest strengths since my return. I didn't acquire the ability to love from just my own efforts; rather, I opened myself up to its possibility and it began to come to me from others. Our love on earth is not as pure or fully developed as God's love. But each time I recalled his love, the memory of it flowed through me again. I became full, and then I felt the desire to express it by sharing it with others. Our oneness, the part of us that is love, is in our cellular memory; it is present, in all of us. It is the single most healing energy we have.

Anything wonderful is made more so if you can share it, and I now wanted to share the knowledge that I had received and learn more about the beliefs of others. I knew that strength could be found among like-minded people, and I began attending two different church groups. In one church I found a spiritual expression of God's love and in the other, a knowledge of God's plan. Together, they began to fill a void in my life. Both churches were blessed with God's love, but the expression of that love was demonstrated in different ways. I found a place for both faiths, balancing the two different belief systems in my heart. I knew from my experience that each church fulfills spiritual needs that perhaps others cannot fulfill. I now experienced the truth of that in my own life. No one church can fulfill everybody's needs at every level; there is no "perfect" religion for all of us. I had been shown that, because we are at various levels of spirituality, any step closer to God is good, so we should never criticize any church or faith where people are seeking God.

Christ's ministry, I understood, is all about loving one another. Nothing comes between us and God's love except what we place there. Our self-righteousness and judgmental attitudes often mask the obstacles we've created that block us from God's love. I could see that I had done this before in my life, and that the judgments I had formed actually hid fears of mine that I didn't want to see. As I nurtured my faith at these two churches, I was careful not to make this mistake again.

God's love is like the sun, constant and shining for us all. And just as the earth rotates around the sun, it is the natural order for us to move away for a season, and then to return closer, but always within the appropriate time. I saw now that when I had moved away, it was often for the purpose of acquiring new tools that could not have been acquired in any other way. When I paid for an experience with pain, caused by the absence of his presence, I internalized the experience and was able to grow more positively from the experience. Coming back to God's presence, I was able to use what I had found to strengthen me and to glorify him in a greater way. But it was always my choice to use the experience as I desired.

When I internalized more of my understanding of God's will for me, I felt a sense of freedom and peace that sank deep into me, like a breath of sweet almond blossoms to my soul. My spirit began to swell again as it had when I first recognized the truth and love that existed with God. Unconditional love and knowledge have no boundaries; there is no "how," "who," "if," or "when." I had feasted at Jesus's feet and experienced the boundless, unconditional love of my creator, my God. Knowledge was poured into me unconditionally, and the joy that brought was beyond compare.

As powerful as these insights from my experience were, I realized it was not yet time to share them, either in church or out. I had seen that it was important that I not interfere with the spiritual beliefs of another by imposing my beliefs on them. We grow best when we progress at our own speed from our current beliefs to greater understanding. By criticizing the faith of others or by using unrighteous judgment, I could act as a stumbling block to others' beliefs, hindering their growth or even taking away what spirituality they have. I could see now that I had made this error in previous attempts to share my experiences. In my zealous desire to be "right" and make others "right" with me, I had impatiently and judgmentally stepped into their path, tripping them, hurting myself, and accomplishing nothing. Now I no longer desired conversion for anyone. I saw that they must desire change for themselves, and I knew that God, our loving Father, would place that in their heart when or if they were ready. When we trust in God, he guides and directs us to further knowledge as we need it. Growth is a process, and when we take time to internalize and understand what we believe, we are more richly blessed; our beliefs radiate in our countenance for all to see. All I needed to do was to share freely what had been given to me and to set the best example of love I could.

God gave me my most glorious opportunity to express my love when our youngest daughter, little Betty, came into our lives, first as a foster child then later as our adopted daughter. She was a gift to me from God, a reminder of the wonders of the spirit world, where I had first seen her spirit and immediately recognized our bond. When she was taken from our foster care to be adopted by relatives of the alcoholic parents from whom she had been removed, I prayed for her return. When I abandoned hope for her return, I prayed for the family who had taken her. It was then that she came back to us, battered by her would-be adoptive parents. As I surrounded her in the healing power of unconditional love, I witnessed the enormous power of God's love when we pass it on to another person. And every time I looked at her angelic face, I was reminded of God's love for me, humbled that he had answered my prayers and grateful he had given me this precious spirit to love unconditionally.

"Love one another," Jesus had said. "If you can do that, all else will be fine." Setting an example of love and knowing that no one has the answer for all gave me greater focus and vision for his will in my life.

The gift of love was freely given to me, but the gift of communicating with him was not. In the spirit world I had been able to express my feelings without using words. Our communication was pure and without effort. Back on this earth, I found no words that could express my thoughts and emotions. I knew that God already knew my heart; he could see my desire for direct contact within it. I left it up to him to show me how.

Then, one night God made it clear to me that our relationship was a two-way street. I was sleeping soundly when I heard a loud voice that brought me awake. As I lay there listening, I did not understand what I had heard and knew only that it was a man's voice. I could see Joe was still sleeping, so it had not been him. I thought it was unusual that the voice had not awakened Joe, who is always more alert at nighttime. Then I heard it again: "Get up and pray." It was now clear that only I heard it. Whether it was God or a messenger I wasn't sure, but there was no doubt that the voice was firm and had authority. I thought of a father's tone when he wants his child to do something, now!

Without hesitation, I hurried out of bed and knelt beside it. I had not been told what to pray about, so I just began silently praying for my family, thinking that one of them must be in need. I finished and returned to bed. It wasn't long before I was awakened a second time and told in that same manner to pray again. Once more I fell to my knees. Having already prayed for my children and other family members, I prayed for the President, church leaders, and anyone else I could think of.

When I mentioned this to Joe the next day, we called around to check on the family. Everyone was fine. We listened to the news and found nothing serious had happened. When the call to pray came again later that week, I went into another room so that I could pray out loud and not disturb Joe. I asked Heavenly Father to reveal to me who I should pray for because I was anxious to be of service. When the answer came back that he just wanted to hear from me and that the prayer was more for my own benefit than anyone else's, I realized that I should have known. I saw that this had always been in my heart, I just wasn't expressing it. From then on, whenever the call came, I just talked to him, unless I was given something or someone specifically to pray for.

I began to think of God as more of a father in my communciations with him. "God" is a way to express the Ultimate Source, the Omnipotence, but the God I met was more like a father, someone personal and loving, not just an authority figure. We talked together as parent and child. I shared with him my joys and fears. I began to thank him for the things in which he expressed himself, which was just about everything. I began to look forward to those times we had and soon found that my talks with him did not have to be at night, on my knees, but that I could have an ongoing communication with him all day long. Often the interruptions of others annoyed me, and I wondered how I could possibly have gone so long without this. I still had more to learn about being mortal, the ways in which, in the flesh, I am weak, but I rejoiced at the lessons God had shown me. Though I was still in the flesh, I was with him again. That was all that mattered.

Spiritual Progression

The spirit continued to manifest itself in me, but it did not fit neatly into the spirituality I associated with religion. As I developed with the knowledge I had been given, such as the details of my near-death experience, I found it hard to share that knowledge with others. The awakening of my spirit, although exciting, was an isolating force. While it led me to the spiritual being within me and brought me closer to God, it also separated me from those with whom I had once shared similar views.

My heightened state of spiritual awareness made me more intense. I became more keenly aware in all my senses, even my taste, touch and smell. My partial loss of hearing added to my sensitivity; generally when one sense is decreased, the others are enhanced. In my case, I began to sense things before they happened. My energy somehow vibrated at a higher level than that of most other people. It seemed that this higher level of energy even affected battery-operated and other electronic devices. When I became excited by any strong emotion, especially love or anger, everything around me reacted. The lights would often brighten or dim, and mechanical things worked differently or simply malfunctioned; other people often became more excitable, too.

Other sensory powers developed in me. At first I "knew" what people thought but did not express verbally. I didn't understand how I accomplished this, and I often felt like an intruder. I was embarrassed at first because I thought I was deliberately accessing a private part of their life. Often I became aware of events that had not yet happened, and I would sometimes frighten my family when I "knew" that something was about to happen in their lives. After I warned them, it usually did. I became like a weather vane to my friends, who looked to me to tell them if things would be all right. I didn't want the responsibility, because we can change some things by choice, and predicting the future of someone else placed me in a role I wanted to avoid.

My awareness continued to increase without any conscious effort on my part, and I soon realized that what I was doing was something I had done "naturally" when I was in the spirit world. I had rejoiced in the wealth of knowledge that was available to me in the library of knowledge in the spirit world. Unlike our libraries on earth, the library of knowledge contained no books. Instead there was a device that functioned like a screen, similar to the one later used by the council of men during my life review. The screen spread out in front of me, as if on a tabletop, and its surface seemed liquid. When I desired knowledge, it would scroll back, and I became a part of that knowledge, internalizing it with all of my senses and with additional senses that we don't have here. I actually experienced what was happening, so that it became a part of me.

I began to refer to my new abilities as Extra Spiritual Progression, others might refer to it as ESP. I realized that I was not only tapping into knowledge contained in the energy fields that surround me, but tapping into the heart and spirit of others. Each of us, I learned, carries in our presence an energy "blueprint" that contains our present thoughts, deeds, and experiences, as well as all of our background and possible future. I had been able to connect with pure knowledge in the spirit world; now I could tap into it on earth and just "know" about a person.

This access into the spirit gave me the opportunity to learn the difference between pure knowledge and perception. The pure truth of everything exists within our cells and our spirit. God had tapped into my spirit, and I into his, when I stood in his presence. What I "knew" about him was that he was pure love, unconditional love. What he "knew" about me, he forgave. God goes beyond the field and "knows" our hearts, our intent.

Our mortal truth is often rationalized, justified, analyzed, processed, and otherwise filtered through the brain before it comes out in our energy fields, and by then it may not be the pure truth. Mediums and channelers, though they may be spiritually sensitive people, receive according to their spiritual growth, using their gifts only within the framework of their perceptions. Because they only "see" what has already been filtered through our conscious or subconscious minds, their readings can be based on deceptive input and therefore not useful to them or us. We can acquire more honest guidance by seeking our answers from God, asking him to place the truth into our hearts.

I saw that everything we express in our energy fields comes from our perception, the filter through which we understand the world. Our perceptions begin to form at birth and continue to develop through childhood; then we continue to express those childhood perceptions, our belief system, for the rest of our lives. What is in a person's heart can often be dramatically different from what comes from their lips. Our beliefs can hold the spirit back from reaching its greatest potential if they inhibit the love that we naturally want to share or if the untruths of remembered pain learned in childhood are not uncovered. We can let go of our impure mortal belief systems by seeking our spiritual selves in our Creator, our Father in Heaven. We *can* do this, but we don't always know how or believe that we can. When we do, we are more open to love.

This insight into others was a difficult gift to live with. The information was invaluable to me, but I had knowledge that I couldn't share with just anyone, and the "knowing" became a heavy burden. I eventually prayed and asked for this ability to be removed or decreased so that I could live more normally and naturally. In his wisdom God did as I asked but told me that I must grow into my gifts. At that point I had not, but I knew he would help me to.

As the spiritual intensity began to decrease, I remembered that God had already quieted or removed our ability to tap into pure knowledge by placing a veil between us when we came to earth. When I was shown the creation of the earth in the spirit world, I saw that we all participated by agreeing to the laws that govern us here. It was then that we mutually agreed that our full access to the pure knowledge of spirit would interfere with our use of free will here on earth. Since we are here to use our will to progress spiritually, we agreed that God would veil us from those gifts on earth. But those gifts do remain, as I saw in my own life, and when we are kept close to the veil it is for his purpose.

The knowledge of what has always been remains in us, as part of his plan for us. Sometimes we call it intuition, at other times, we call it inspiration. When we follow our hearts, when we are in tune and balanced, and when we listen to the still inner voice within us . . . we "know." These gifts and abilities are stored in our cells—our cellular memory—and they include the experiences and lessons learned by our ancestors, which are also imprinted in every cell of our body. We pass those memories to our children and then to later generations; these include both genetic and spiritual memories. The spiritual memory is coded during our preexistence with God, and it contains the senses and abilities that I was able to use in the spirit world—in the library and in my nonverbal communication with any number of spirits—and was able to use again after I returned.

To use these gifts on earth, we tune into the spiritual power that is within us. That higher source can access all our cellular memory; it is the divine part of us. As God's spiritual children, we are a part of him. God is love, and love is in us, and that is our source of energy. It is natural for us to desire to love and to be loved. Sometimes we lose our ability to love, because it has been overshadowed by struggle, despair, anguish, and fears. But it is still there in our memory to be recalled when we are ready.

As my beliefs were challenged, both by my near-death

experience and my enhanced abilities, the unconditional love stored in my cells began to awaken. My spirit stirred, remembering the love I had felt in the presence of Jesus and how that love filled me to overflowing and I grew. Now my cells recalled an abundance of love, *unconditional* love, and my greatest challenge was to learn to use that love for a mission that was not totally revealed to me.

My spirit also opened to memories that I could not understand, information I didn't know I carried and didn't see how I could use. This awakening information was the knowledge given to me by my Native American ancestors. Prior to my near-death experience, I had not been taught about my Native American ancestry. There was little mention of it at the Indian schools of my youth and even less in my home. My parents were proud of the fact that their children were half white, and my two marriages to white men further reduced my connection and my children's connection to our heritage.

My cellular awakening began to change that, because my senses were awakening to that part of my ancestry. I was drawn to the outdoors, and I had an overwhelming need to be in nature, away from the artificial surroundings of the house. I began camping and fishing, and rediscovering the skills of the outdoor life I had forgotten from my childhood. I was awakened to memories of the distant past, of things that I could not have known. I could recall Native American history, sensing it, feeling it . . . the pure knowledge of it that I had carried in my cells. Now I came to trust my spiritual progression more than anything else, not only the awakening of my Native American cell memory, but my expanding knowledge of God that I knew would be of service for the work that lay ahead.

The Mother's Prayer

With little Betty's schedule, I was in the habit of going to bed at a regular hour, but tonight was unusual. I was restless. I couldn't go to sleep and stayed up until about three o'clock in the morning.

When I went to bed, my husband had left his police scanner on. He frequently had it on at night, often falling asleep as he listened to the activities of our son Joe Jr., who was a police officer in a rural area nearby. Young Joe worked days as well, so I didn't know if he was working tonight.

It bothered me to listen to the scanner, so I would normally turn it off if I went to bed after my husband. But this night, I got into bed without turning off the

56

scanner, and I was finally drifting off to sleep when I heard my son's voice on the radio. He was requesting help. I had often heard him do that before, because in his area, officers worked without partners. But this time there was a tone in Joe's voice that immediately alerted me that he was in danger.

I woke up my husband, told him what I had heard, and asked him to stay by the scanner. Joseph was in trouble. Quickly I ran outside to the place by the back porch where I always prayed. As I began to pray, something inside of me said, "Pray, and pray hard." Still not knowing what the danger might be, I began to pray. I asked God to surround him with the warring angels. I had learned about these angels during my experience, and I knew that I could call on them. And I needed them now. I had also watched the "mothers' prayers" and seen that they reached into heaven like bright beacons of light. I knew that the mothers' prayers were the greatest prayers ever heard, and I reminded God that I remembered this.

I prayed, "Father, for some reason your help is needed, and it's needed now. If it is your will that this be done, I call down the warring angels to surround him and to protect him." Not wanting to interrupt my prayers, but desperately wanting to know what was going on, I ran back into the house to hear if Joe Sr. had learned anything. There was no word of Joe on the radio, so I called my son's precinct. They told me that they did not have any further news, but that other officers had been dispatched. "I know my son is in trouble," I told them. "Please, the minute that you hear anything, I want a report back." And then I ran back outside and continued to pray.

It was an hour before we knew he was safe and several hours before Joe filled me in on what had happened to him. He had been on a country road, pursuing a speeding car that was trying to get away from him. The driver had sped over a hill and tried to make a quick U-turn to throw my son off. But the turn wasn't fast enough to pull out of Joe's way as he came down the hill, and the two cars collided.

On impact, the air bag in Joe's car opened and saved his life. Joe hadn't been driving his usual car, which was in the repair shop. His usual car didn't have an air bag.

Joe had called for backup immediately after the collision. He later told me that his first thought was "Somehow I know that Mom is praying for me." Bleeding profusely, the driver had gotten out of his car and attacked my son as he was on the car radio. They fought for eight minutes until the other police officers and medics were able to get there. The driver was so violent that it took eight of them to hold him down.

Joe was taken to the hospital when they found him covered with blood, but after he was cleaned up, they discovered that none of the blood was his. Other than stiff muscles and swollen knees that had connected with the dashboard underneath the air bag, there was nothing wrong with him. They later learned that the driver had been on a high dose of a drug called angel dust, or PCP.

Joe called me from the station as soon as he could. "You know, Mom, right after I finished calling the station, I felt your prayers," he told me. "Then I thought, 'No way, Mom would be asleep.' But something inside of me said, 'No, she's not, she's commissioning the Lord right now for your safety.' Were you up at that time praying for me? The thought that you were kept me going."

"Yes," I answered, "and you can believe that I said the mother's prayer and God could not refuse me."

Many times since this incident my children have brought me to my knees to pray the mother's prayer. Not all of my prayers were answered as immediately as this one, but I knew that God heard them and the answer was on its way.

There were other times during the refining of my spirit that I was reminded of God's boundless might and the awesome power of prayer. There were times, too, that I was painfully reminded of my mortality and the mortality of the ones that I loved. I had often read in the Bible that God gives us only what we can handle, but sometimes I felt that he had given me more than my share.

My father's ill health had placed him in my care for the

long term. Then Joe suddenly became ill with a virus that attacked his heart, and he was put into intensive care. I called our children and we gathered at our home. All of them could come except for our son Glenn, a sergeant in the Marine Corps, who was stationed in Saudi Arabia during the Gulf War.

The living room coffee table was the centerpiece for our family gatherings for prayer. We gathered again, this time to pray for my husband, Joe, who I had just been told would probably not live through the night. When we had all knelt around the table, I told them that before we prayed for their father's healing, we needed to be specific. We agreed that we did not want to pray for his life to be spared if he was going to have to live in a condition that he would find unbearable. And, since we would be praying for God's will to be done, we also needed to accept however God chose to return him to us. With all in agreement, we prayed in turn, each person praying specifically and claiming a part of his healing as each one felt inspired to do. When we finished praying, we shared our feelings and we "knew" that God was going to heal Joe. We returned to the hospital—and within hours he became better.

Joe's heart, lungs, kidneys, and other organs had been seriously damaged by the virus, and his doctors couldn't believe that he continued to live after their last prognosis. We knew that God had healed him, but it was going to take a while for his body to regain strength.

Joe's healing continued in the intensive care unit for sixteen days. Dad's health had worsened, and his requirements kept me running back and forth to the hospital, then to my father's home, as I prepared to move him into our house. His doctor had informed us that his heart was getting weaker. The situation was becoming very stressful, and I had asked friends and family to include us in their prayers, also adding all of our names to the prayer hot lines that I had used before. I knew that the power of prayer is the greatest gift that we have for any situation.

Before Joe recovered, I received a call from my son Glenn's wife, Kelly, informing me that Glenn had been wounded in the desert on his way to Kuwait. He was hospitalized in Dhahran with a head injury, a crushed skull, and his chances for recovery did not look good.

I was stunned. I felt that God had totally turned away from me. I truly had thought that I was doing everything he wanted me to do. I was struggling with the experience, trying to balance my spirituality, working through many of my problems. It just seemed like an endless series of changes in my family, and I felt I had to face them all without the support of my father, my husband, *or* my eldest son.

Before he left for Saudi Arabia, Glenn had shared with me his feeling that something like this would happen. He called me and asked if I had any feeling about his returning to his wife and child. I sensed that he would have some difficulty, but I also felt that he would be okay. Not wanting to concern him just before he went, I said nothing.

Now I felt destitute, deserted, and terribly alone, with more than I could manage. And as for God, this time I felt that he was asking too much of me. I felt angry. How could he allow this to happen to me! To my family! We had done nothing but serve him, and we trusted in his will in our lives. We had watched Joe suffer and begin slowly to heal; couldn't God have left it at that?

When I learned that Glenn's surgery would require a tremendously skilled surgeon and that the hospital in Dhahran could not provide the care he needed, I ran outside to the place that I prayed. I was screaming. And for the first time in my life I prayed a prayer that I have never prayed before or since. Nor do I ever wish to pray this kind of prayer again. I just didn't have the right words to express to God my disappointment in his will for me or my family. When he would awaken me during the night and ask me to pray, I would do it without question. To me the most important thing was obedience. I prayed for as long as my spirit would ask me to pray. And I didn't know what I was praying for or who I praying for. I just did as I was told and stayed on my knees until the spirit moved me to quit.

But this night, as I looked up into the heavens, I screamed at him from the depths of my soul, "What in the hell is going on, God?" I challenged him. "You said that you wouldn't give us more than we could bear. Well, you've stretched it too far this time! This *is* more than I can bear. I can't stand it anymore. What do you want of me!!"

I didn't ask him for help this time. I demanded he take away the burden, the pain. "I've just had enough," I raged. "You think I'm much stronger than I am. I'm not! I don't want to be tested anymore. I'm done. I've had it up to here. First my father, then my husband, now my son . . . You think I'm strong . . . Well, I'm not! What do you think of that!!"

I fell to my knees—not to worship him this time and not to communicate with him, either. I felt that he was destroying me by asking too much, and I couldn't take anymore. I just wanted him to know about it—straight from my heart.

A couple of days later, I learned what God had done. A surgeon had *just arrived* in Dhahran from *our* medical center where our family received health care. He had been called to active duty and assigned to the hospital where Glenn was, and he "just happened" to be a brain surgeon who specialized in the type of surgery my son needed. Everything that Glenn needed God had already provided for him. The miracles surrounding this incident overwhelmed me—and still do—and I was once again ashamed of my lack of trust in God. I thought he was doing nothing but watch me suffer, when he had already taken care of my needs. Once again I had trusted in what I could see and not in the unseen. I had leaned on arms of flesh for my support and comfort, on my father, husband, and son, when what God showed me was that they, too, are mortal and he alone is God. The most important thing I needed to learn to do was to totally lean on him. I saw that all three of these men in my life could be removed at any point, but God, my eternal Father, would always there. He had again taught me to communicate with him. I could count on that communication, and even though it seemed sometimes just one-way, I knew that he heard. He had brought me to that point, reminding me again of where he was to be in my life, and that was first. I asked his forgiveness, and I thanked him for the blessings that I received during my trials of faith. Then I asked him for the courage to go on.

My husband healed, and although he still has some health problems, he has been a blessing to all of the family and has seen and enjoyed many more grandchildren. My son survived his surgeries and became a father once more; in three years, he will retire from the service that he loves. And as for my father, he lived another year and brought a lot of joy to my family, allowing us to be of service to him, teaching us many lessons we might not otherwise have learned. So . . . I was blessed. In my darkest hour, the greatest lesson was being taught me. I knew now that I was willing to lean only on God, completely.

The First Call

My children were on their own except for little Betty, and she was doing well in school. Despite having already raised six children, I could not suppress the drive to do more. I was approaching fifty, and the arrival of my sixth grandchild was yet another sign that the next generation would be taking my place, but I could not deny the energy that I was experiencing.

After many years of prayer for God's guidance in my life, my faith and trust in him were solid, and I knew that any day he would direct me to new areas of growth if I continued to follow him. I was working as a volunteer at a cancer research center, but I felt I had to do more. And then it happened, as this type of thing always does, without warning. I received a call from a friend who had sought out counseling for sexual abuse that had kept her depressed for years. She was now seeking help again, but this time she wanted to try a different technique—hypnotherapy. She asked me if I would sit in on a session with her. She trusted the therapist but did not want to be alone on her first visit. I went along, and as the session progressed I began to get a warm feeling in my body that filled me with incredible excitement. As the therapist guided my friend into regression, I "knew" where to take it from there. It was almost more than I could bear to just sit there and listen and remain an observer. My friend began to weep as she discovered the hidden pain. Though qualified, the therapist seemed at a loss as to where to guide my friend from there, so she began to wrap up the session. My "knowing" finally had to be expressed. Not wanting to interrupt the moment, I wrote the therapist a note asking if I could help and added my suggestions. She agreed and asked for my friend's approval. With that I went to work directing my friend to her wounded spirit. I felt spiritually guided during that session in a way that I had not experienced before. I knew I had a new calling, and I was eager to do whatever it would take to accomplish it.

I discovered that one of the oldest schools in the world that taught hypnotherapy was right here in my area, and I immediately enrolled. I quickly understood that much of what I had previously thought about hypnosis was full of old wives' tales and superstitions. I learned that hypnosis is a state of being that we find ourselves in daily, a time of complete, relaxed focus in which time passes without our being aware of it. I was attracted to the way that a good therapist forgoes his or her own ego to work with the beliefs of the client, transmitting healing energy to the spiritual essence of the patient, tapping into the energy of love, which, along with prayer, is among the most powerful tools that we have for recovery.

During my study and training, I had the wonderful experience of supporting my daughter Donna through the delivery of her first child. Her use of hypnosis during her labor, instead of using drugs or medicine, astounded her doctor and nurses. This was the first time hypnosis was ever used in that hospital, and I was invited to come back again.

Soon after I graduated, I opened my very own clinic. That day I stood back and looked at the sign that said I was an expert at something. My becoming a hypnotherapist was the fulfillment of a dream that some women might only wish for. My office became my private place, shared by no one, and I began to love being there more than anywhere else in the world. I was me here—just me, with the talents that God gave me. I had developed those talents (I gave myself that much credit), and I planned to use them to help others. But the feelings of pride were just too irresistible, and I enjoyed every moment of them.

My clientele grew rapidly. I began to receive doctor referrals, and the prestige of that increased my business even more. I worked long hours, fitting in some clients in the evening, after little Betty was settled down. She was eight years old when I first began work, and she liked to come to the office after school. She enjoyed sitting in my inner office and doing her homework or helping me with small chores when I didn't have an appointment.

Then one day I saw an ad in the paper from a researcher who was looking for participants for a study on near-death experiences. I anxiously called the researcher and set up an appointment. When I shared my near-death experience with him, it stirred up emotions in me that I had not realized were so intense. I sobbed uncontrollably as I recounted the events that led up to and occurred during and after the experience.

The researcher published my story along with others in an article that caught the attention of a local newsman. He called to ask for an interview for a television show he wanted to do on the subject. Again, as the interview proceeded, my emotions could not be held back. The film that was produced that day was never used, for reasons only the filmmakers know. But the release of energy from my broken heart and the homesickness for the home of my spirit overwhelmed me for days.

Soon after, I read in the newspaper of monthly meetings for people who had had a near-death experience.

The group was called the International Association for Near-Death Studies, more popularly known as IANDS. On attending my first meeting, I learned that the organization was becoming worldwide and the group in my area was currently the largest. When I left the meeting that afternoon, I felt as I imagined a person who had attended their first AA meeting or a Christian revival would feel. My feet barely touched the ground, I felt so lifted and alive!

My life was full, I had my new career, and little Betty was a blessing I could never have comprehended before. Now I could not imagine not having her with me. Joe was looking forward to retirement, which was just five short years away, and the older children, as they grew from child to adult to spouse to parent, held my interest fully. I felt that after all these years of adjusting, a change in spirit had finally happened. I was content and richly blessed by God.

Then, one Saturday afternoon, I was driving home from visiting with a friend, listening to a favorite tape of beautiful piano music. I had known since my experience that no music on earth can compare to the vastness and strength of the songs of God's praise that I heard in the spirit world. Having basked in the vast cosmic song that soothed and comforted me, I knew, also, that music can be a source of great healing—as well as the opposite. Since my return, I had tried to avoid music that takes its listeners to a place of darkness and sought out music that was energized by the power of light and love. I was stimulated by the energy of the music in the car that afternoon, and I had my hand up, directing it, in full body movement as an orchestra director.

I still had my hand up when there was a sudden pause and all time seemed to stand still. From a voice that resonated within me, I received a message that came so strongly it jarred me for hours. The message came as a direct command.

"Betty, it is time. You must share with the world the message of God's love. Set up a meeting place that is open to all. Advertise it in the newspaper. All who come will be sent. Go there with your heart, listen, and speak from it."

I knew with a perfect knowing that my mission was just beginning. The message left no room for misinterpretation. It was simple and direct. God had given me time to internalize the knowledge given to me; now he was ready for me to use it. Once home, I immediately called my friend Nancy and told her what I had been instructed to do. "Honey," she said softly, "I was waiting for this to happen. Tell me what to do and I will help you do it."

Four days later I sat in the office of the local newspaper. All I wanted was a small ad mentioning a local person wants to share an interesting subject; come if you feel like it. I was given a reporter instead. He was kind and listened patiently as I told him about my experience.

When the paper came out, I was astonished to see that he had written a two-page article; the picture of me took up a quarter of the front page! This had all happened so fast that I had not had time to tell many of my friends. Some of them had never heard that I had had a near-death experience.

Nancy chose a library for the meeting and helped put together flyers. The only time available on the library's calendar was just before Mother's Day. I quickly took that time because I thought most people would be out of town that weekend, and I was beginning to feel nervous about the exposure being so close to home. When the day came, I arrived late at the library, and I could not believe the crowded parking lot. People were rushing into the building and then being sent back out. I squeezed through the crowd and found that the small room we were using was packed. There were people everywhere, sitting on the floor, lined up against the wall, and filling the hallway.

I began to speak, and as I started sharing my experience, I felt a hush of peace surround me. I knew that I was doing what I was supposed to do, and that God was caring for my other concerns while he used me here. We took some time to hear the special stories of those who wanted to share. Some spoke of their pain, and they wondered where God was when it happened. But their willingness to seek God was evident in their spirits, and the desire for his love was, too. There was not a dry eye when the meeting was over. People from every walk of life had attended. God had sent them as he told me he would. There was no doubt left in me now that he keeps his word; I have learned that each step of the way. As I shook the hands of those who were leaving, my love for them filled me, and I couldn't help but wonder why I had been so reluctant to do this before.

I continued working at my clinic with a desire to open another one on the other side of the city. I had great plans and I knew that they would work. I was also caring for my father, who was having some difficulty after quadruple bypass surgery; he then lived with my stepmother, who was also ill. Although caring for them meant preparing six meals a day—three at their home, three at mine—and double the cleaning, washing, shopping, and doctor appointments, I loved every minute that God gave me to be with them. Not that all of those moments were good; often, they were not. But he gave me enough moments to leave me many memories of ones that I did enjoy.

Word of mouth about my first presentation spread rapidly, and I started to receive many calls from grief groups and requests from various church groups to speak at their meetings. I was also called to many bedsides where I would share my experience to comfort the dying as they passed. Sometimes, when they could talk, they would share their own experience with meeting their loved ones or God.

After I had celebrated the third year in my clinic and had the wonderful experience of assisting in the birth of another grandchild, I began to make plans to expand my business and perhaps teach what I had learned. Joe and the family—even my father, sick as he was—were excited for me, too. My children began to help me out on my busier days when they could, filling in as receptionist on the weekends and doing my backed up paperwork. I often joked that before I started this work, the only filing I ever did was my fingernails. We all laughed, but the truth is, I never understood that process. Everything I filed, I filed under the letter *W* for "Why in the heck did I put that here!" There was an energy, a joyfulness, a family united in Mom's happiness, and I loved every minute of it.

To Say Good-bye

God had one more lesson for me to learn before I was to take his message any further.

My father was in my personal care for the last five years of his life, during the last two of which he was very ill with diabetes and heart problems. Dad lived until he was eighty-three years old, which was young compared to his parents. All his life he had lived with a sturdy, simple faith. He had a beautiful voice and used it to sing all the hymns he had been taught as a child; "The Old Rugged Cross" and "Beyond the Sunset" were our favorites for him to sing.

As father and daughter, our friendship and love for each other extended beyond this earth. But Dad's religious upbringing prevented us from discussing what I knew of this bond. Although Dad believed in God and believed that we live with God after death, we could never talk about my near-death experience and the lessons I learned from it. To Dad, the life hereafter was one of God's mysteries and was best left at that. Not that I felt he needed to hear the message I had been given. In my eyes, no one was more deserving of God's love than my dad; nothing had to be spelled out to him about love or faith, and he lived the walk of kindness and charity.

When I moved Dad into our home, I cut back on my hours at my clinic, but he was so proud of my having the clinic that I didn't give it up entirely; he wanted me to work, and he needed to feel that he could tend to his own needs the few hours I was away. I learned many valuable lessons as I cared for him. It is often easy for parents and children to switch roles when the parent gets older, and I began to feel like his parent. I eventually came to realize, though, that he was still my teacher, and I the student, but I didn't truly understand that until after he died. He did his best not to be too demanding of my time, but as his health deteriorated and he became more reliant on me, he was transformed from a tall, strong, healthy man to an invalid in a wheelchair. His mind, though, was still sharp and clear even as his body aged. Dad used to comment on how he felt trapped inside the body of an old man, and I could relate to that feeling of being trapped: I had felt that way when my spirit was returned to my physical body.

I tried to keep Dad's spirits high, but I could not roll back the years and give him back his youth and good health. When I learned that I could not be all and do all for him, it hurt me. I loved him so much and I wanted him to be happy and well. I realized that as only one of his ten children, I could bring him just one ray of sunshine, and that reminded me of my Father in heaven, who has more children than can be counted. Not a single one of his children is more important than the others—even though we might think that we are.

Because Dad and I were so close, and because of the severity of my deep depression years before, my brothers and sisters worried about how I would handle Dad's death. When they could speak to me alone, they would voice their concern, telling me that I needed to plan for when Dad left us. I had thought about that, too, remembering my depression and feelings of loss after I come back from the spirit world. The despair and homesickness had almost destroyed me back then. I prayed that would never happen to me again.

Dreams have always been an important part of my expanded awareness of the spiritual realm. They can provide a gateway for communication from our loved ones in the spirit world and can also connect us with our higher self and God, affording us an opportunity to receive messages in the conscious mind. Often our dreams are full of symbolism, but they are our own symbols, some so uniquely our own that only the dreamer has the key to them.

Two weeks before my father's death, I had a dream that concerned me. I was standing near a gate that opened into a garden. I knew that a birthday party was about to take place and I was in charge of it. Other family members came and I asked them to wait by the gate until I found out if everything was ready. I went through the gate and into the house. On a table I saw the most beautiful birthday cake. As decoration on the cake, a cute little porcelain angel was poised over a candle. Joe asked if I wanted to see how the cake worked before the others saw it, and I said, "Yes!" He lit the candle and stood back so that I could see. The angel came to life, fluttering his wings, and then smiled at me as though looking for approval. Then the angel leaned over the candle and blew out the flame with an audible puff. I clapped my hands with delight and begged Joe, "Do it again!" Joe lit the candle once more and the angel moved as it had before. "Once more, please." I laughed, and Joe lit the candle for the third time, the angel puffing the flame out one last time. It delighted me so that I wanted more, but I was interrupted by four reporters, one of whom held a clipboard in his hands and asked me for our family's history, explaining that the birthday celebration was going to be reported in the newspaper. The rest of the family was led in, but my daughter Donna had not yet arrived. I called her and told her that we would wait, but to hurry before it was too late. And then it was over.

I felt anxious about this dream as soon as I was awake. As cute as the angel had been, I understood that this was a dream of premonition, and that I had looked symbolically into the future. Little Betty's birthday was on the twenty-first, which was one week away, so I decided to watch her a little more closely. I was greatly relieved when her birthday came and went without incident.

Within little more than a week, I sat rocking in anguish on my bed, tears rolling down my face as I repeated to myself, "I should have known, I should have known." I had always "known" things before, but not this time. Although I had been alerted to the possibility of something happening, I hadn't known what it would be. I know that God often "hides" things from people for a reason, and I guessed now that this was one of those times. As I reached for another tissue, I noticed that I had left my journal on the night stand. I opened the journal, deciding to make a few notes about the day when my eyes caught the entry for July 26, 1991.

"Last night I had a vision of Momma," I read. "She said that she needed to tell me something important. Mom looked young and beautiful, her hair was rolled back in a forties hairstyle. She smiled often and was extremely happy. I couldn't take my eyes off of her, I love her so much! After a nice visit, she left." Then, written in bold letters under that entry, I had written, "I don't remember what we talked about! darn!! Oh, well, I felt comforted by her presence."

As I sat there reading, I looked in the journal for other clues, but after that last entry, my journal was blank. I had been busy wrapping up some business at my office for the weekend, and those two days had left me too tired to do much else, although I remembered that the day before, which was a Saturday, had been an unusual day worth noting. After dinner I had sat with Dad and watched television. He was in a quiet mood but enjoyed his favorite program. After the show I reminded him that in the morning we were going to church with my sister Dorothy. I wanted to help him with his bath before I went to bed. Usually the mention of a bath put my father in the worst of moods. He hated the fact that he was dependent on me for his personal care, but he refused outside help because he was a very modest man.

Dad was strangely different this night, kind of light-hearted and fun. He used to always be this way, and I enjoyed him more when he was. He asked me if I could give him a haircut before his bath. I had been his barber for twenty-four years, so that didn't seem strange, but all this energy and interest in his grooming was.

As I began to trim the hair around his ears, he said, "Tighten it up good on the sides, Betty, I won't be needing another haircut." I thought I had misunderstood him, so I said nothing. After Dad's bath, and before

I could ask him if I could put lotion on his dry skin, he asked me if I would. My offers in the past had always brought on an argument, but again, this night was different. I put lotion on his legs, arms, and back as we talked about many pleasant things. He was happy and pleasing to be with, so I wanted to stay in his room longer than I usually did. Not wanting to end our visit, I reluctantly tucked him in bed and kissed him good night. As I closed his door, I thanked God for this beautiful evening with Dad. Lately I had noticed that these moments were getting fewer and farther between.

After church the next day, Dad, Dorothy, our friend Mike, and I went to have lunch, as was our habit each Sunday. Dad's mood had not changed. He was in a rare form of excitement; he joked and laughed often and got kidded about his spiffy Sunday clothes and fresh haircut. At the table the waitress poured coffee and gave us our menus. Dad was laughing with my sister Dorothy about something he had heard at church. I was reading the menu when I heard Dad asking me, "Betty, would you hand me the sugar." I reached for the sugar, then turned back toward Dad to hand it to him. In that short time, his head had bowed and his eyes were closed. "Dad," I asked, "are you okay?" When he didn't answer, I threw back my chair and ran to him. Standing behind Dad, I wrapped my arms around him and felt his body relax in my embrace. "Dad!" I wanted to shout, "No, no, Dad!" but I whispered to him instead. "Please, not now, get back into your body, Dad. I know that you are still here, somewhere; now, please . . . get back in!" The restaurant was full with the Sunday afternoon crowd, but that didn't bother me. I wasn't sure what they thought of my comments, but I knew that Dad heard me, and he was the one I was addressing anyway. "Dad," I continued, "you can't go now, the family reunion is only two weeks away."

The family reunion. Our very first one. Dad and I had talked about it just last night as I rubbed his back. He was excited and couldn't wait to see all his children together again. I thought about the reunion that I had had during my near-death experience. To me, it had been the most wonderful time ever. Everyone that I loved who had passed on before me was there; many friends that I had forgotten while on earth but had known in eternity were there, too.

I heard a puff escape from Dad's lips. It was a sound that I had heard before not so long ago. Then I heard a second one and then a third! The dream I had had just two weeks ago began to unfold for me now. The birthday, the angel, three puffs, family waiting. I wondered about the reporters as I gently slid Dad from his chair; his body had become too heavy for me to hold. I sat on the floor with his head resting in my lap and rocked him, loving him. He was gone, just like that. I had felt for a pulse, he had none, I heard Dorothy praying, and someone called 911. Minutes after being called, four men arrived, one with a clipboard in his hand. "Your mysteries are never ending, Heavenly Father!" I thought as the rest of this story unfolded; he was about to ask me for family history. "I'll need some information," he said. "What is the history of your father's health?"

They worked feverishly on Dad as they rushed him to the hospital. Some time back, Dad's doctor had asked us what we intended to do if Dad had problems while at home. The doctor had told my father that his heart had an irregular beat and the bottom half was no longer working, creating greater work for the upper part. After talking it over, Dad and I decided that because of his other health problems, should his heart stop beating, I would not call for aid. In this case, I had no choice. Dad would have preferred not to have had the emergency care.

In the hospital he was hooked up to a ventilator that began to breathe for him, and the doctors had started his heart again. But I knew that Dad was not in his body—he was there with us, but in spirit this time. After talking to Dad's doctor about his wishes not to be kept alive by these methods, we made the decision to remove the ventilator and other life-extending machines.

The family members who could come gathered together when the machines were turned off. All were on time except Donna. Just as I had experienced in my dream, I called Donna to tell her that if she did not hurry she would be too late. When she arrived, we stood over Dad as the machines were turned off. With all of us holding hands, we circled the bed and sang Dad's favorite songs to him. The room was full of those he had loved; were he able to communicate his gratitude, I knew he would. I stood at the head of his bed, holding his hand. I just wanted to say good-bye to him physically one last time. As the nurse came for her final check, I saw Dad's eyes open just for a moment, or maybe I just thought that they did. But his blue-gray eyes looked into mine, and I felt his spirit in them, and I "knew" he had come back just long enough to say good-bye. "Daddy," I whispered, "it's time for you to go. We love you and we'll join you soon. Now, go to the light."

The Final Call

My Dad's death was a great loss to all of us, but especially to me. I felt the absence of his daily presence. I was aware of how much time I had spent with him, during which he was the focus of my attention; even in those hours when he wasn't, I realized, his comfort had always been on my mind. That time was suddenly open now, and I missed him terribly. But I did not grieve.

The events of his death removed any doubts I had had about the divine plan that our leaving this world for the spirit world fulfills. I had seen it firsthand. I knew Dad was in a place of love and light, relieved of his physical pain and weaknesses. There was no reason to grieve for that.

I threw myself into my life, filling the time that was suddenly there to be filled. My family needed me more than ever; a son and a daughter were going through a divorce, and little Betty was of course still the light of my life. I strengthened my commitment to my clinic, taking on help in hopes of expanding its capacity, doing service by helping more and more patients find the healing power within themselves. And I continued to share my near-death experience, both in presentations and in my hospital volunteer work. The loss of my father was always present, but my life was full. I thought I was living true to God's will for me.

Then one night I was awakened from sleep. I felt the presence of angels around me. It wasn't the stillness I had experienced before, the "knowing" feeling of "All is well . . . go back to sleep." This was intense, a feeling of deeper purpose. My surroundings seemed to fade, and I suddenly found myself remembering a vision that had been given to me three years before. I was on a large ship. The ship was filled with all the people in the world. There was a lot of gaiety in the middle of the ship, where people were drinking and dancing. The people surrounding them joined in on occasion, but otherwise were less involved. As I continued to look around, I saw that the two rows of people along the edge of the ship were more serious-minded in appearance.

The outside row wore no smiles at all, but looked deeply concerned. Every now and then they would look out toward the sea and then lean inward and whisper into the ears of those in the inner rows. It was a curious behavior. When I glanced directly behind me, I noticed that I was looking straight into the sea and that I was one of those on the outer edge of the ship.

The sea suddenly became turbulent. The water's color went from a dark blue to an angry, muddy brown. I looked over my right shoulder and saw the edge of the earth, and noticed that the ship was being tossed in its direction. I tried screaming out, but no one could hear me—the laughter from the middle of the ship was too loud. I began to pray, clasping my hands together tightly until they hurt. "Father, oh, Father," I prayed, "save us. Many have not learned of your love, how could they behave other than they do?" The sky roared with thunder and lightning, and the ship began to rock and turn until we were moving sideways. I looked again toward the sea and saw that we had come to the edge of the world.

The people along the outer edge of the ship began to pray as I was, crying out to God in loud pleas. The ones who had been laughing, stopped. They now began to scream out, begging God to spare them. The sky, though still blackened with heavy clouds, scrolled back to expose the brightest light imaginable, and we saw the wonders of heaven. We "knew" that God wanted to show us these things but could not do so without getting our full attention. He wanted us to be spared a disastrous end. He wanted us to know that he cared for us, and that he loved us.

The ship stopped moving sideways and turned to reverse itself. The sky suddenly became clear, and the water smoothed, then turned blue again. I knelt and began to thank and praise God for allowing me to live long enough to see this incredible miracle. The others along the ship's outer edge praised God as I did, and a ripple effect of our prayers of praise and thanks spread inward, until the majority of people aboard ship were worshipping God. It wasn't long, though, before the sounds of worship changed, and the dancing and loud music began again. I looked at the men and women around the edge of the ship, and I knew that God had placed them there as warring angels who had knowledge and faith in God. These earthly angels, through their prayers and efforts, would do battle against Satan. They were just people like me, who believed in God and loved him enough to give their lives to his service. As I looked at them, I knew them, and they me. There were many thousands of us there.

The vision closed, and I lay in bed, thanking God still. I slept for a while, perhaps an hour or two. Then I was awakened once more. I heard a voice that commanded me to lie completely still and not move. My eyes were open, and I blinked them when I needed to; other than that, I made no movement. A stream of words began to flow in front of my eyes. I could see each word spelled out, like a ticker tape, letter for letter each chapter of the book that I was told I would write.

The alarm rang: it was 6:30, and Joe awoke and turned it off. It was our usual time to get up and get ready for work. I had appointments, but I dared not disrupt what I was experiencing. When Joe went to shake me, he noticed that I was awake. He stood there startled for a moment, watching my unusual behavior. I waved him off with my hand, trying to warn him not to disturb me, but it was too late; with that movement, the words stopped flowing. I lay there for a while and tried to understand what had happened.

Joe and I talked that morning and then later that evening about the unusual occurrence. He wasn't as concerned as I was, just sorry that he had interrupted me. I knew that what had happened that morning was real; it was just as clear to me as anything else. But I wasn't sure why it was happening to me now. I had lived these past nineteen years wondering about my experience with death and the spirit world, trying to understand its complete meaning in my life. I was willing to do my part, whatever that was. But why me? And why now!

The next morning I was awakened again. The message was the same as the day before. I was to lie still, not move, and the ticker tape of words began once more. I don't know what time the message started, but I heard the alarm go off again. Joe moved to turn it off, then to awaken me. This time he moved more slowly, then, seeing me lying there not moving with my eyes wide open, he moved quietly out of the bed and left the room. When the words stopped flowing, I had to quickly get out of bed to shower, dress and make it to the office in time for my first appointment. I never recalled a single word after the flow of words had stopped and I moved. However, as the words were fed into my mind, I knew exactly what was being written. I had seen in the spirit world that all material things were created first in spirit; then we bring them to physical reality with the tools and the gifts God gave us. God has always used what has always been. I knew that that was happening to me now. Often my thoughts were still on a particular idea or subject, while the book continued to be written before my eyes. I saw it from cover to cover. Over a period of days this continued to happen to me. Each day was the same, and I did not move until the entire book was given to me in this peculiar fashion.

I thought back to a vision of the world I had been given shortly after the experience, a vision that had mystified me ever since, but that I suddenly saw in a new light. I had been told by the spirit that my experience in God's world had to be shared with all faiths, that it was generically given. I was shown a panoramic view of the earth suspended in space. Then, on earth, I saw what appeared to be a giant octopus, its tentacles poised as if it was choosing where they would land. Then, with an audible smack, they landed one by one, with great force. When they had all attached themselves, the octopus pulled its body all over the globe, until the entire world had been covered. This was incomprehensible to me, but what followed was simply beautiful: The octopus left in its wake a shimmering, blue-green liquid. In a short time, the liquid had coated the world, and the blue-green, vibrating light glowed upon all of the earth's surface. I was still not in tune with its meaning, but I watched in awe.

Now it was explained to me. I had seen my book, my attempt to share God's message, as it first reached the cities that would be the catapults to launch the book into the world. The film was the healing balm of God's love that would reach all of those who feared him. The book would cover the world with God's love; I was to write it, and the time had come.

Embraced by the Light

*W*ith my first public presentation, the ripple effect of getting out the message that would become *Embraced* was set into motion. I was soon speaking at churches, grief groups, wherever those who had heard of my experience would ask me. At one of those churches, the audience included a woman who had been asked by a psychiatrist friend if she would take notes. She arrived with her tape recorder and note pads, and she put together some notes. But she didn't stop there; this had become a driving energy for her, so she attended two more speaking engagements and took more notes. She wanted to share them with her family, and when she graciously contacted me for permission, she sent me a set just to see if they were correct. When I checked over the notes, which were correct, I asked her to add my phone number, inviting her parents to call me if they had any questions.

What I didn't know was that her family was large and that they would copy the notes and send them out to more relatives and friends, who sent out copies to their relatives and friends, and so on. As the copies grew fainter, people often retyped them—sometimes shorter versions, sometimes longer—and as the message rippled out even further, several versions began circulating. But all of them had my phone number right, and I received phone call after phone call, literally from around the world, as the notes brought their message to an ever-expanding circle. These people would soon have a different role to play when the book was published, as important participants in the process of getting the book out into the world.

It was clear that the time had come for the message I had been given to be spread farther than I could do on my own, in person. God saw to it that it happened. I had tried to write about my experience several years before, prior to the spirit telling me it was time, and I soon found it too difficult to continue. It wasn't yet time; I was pushing ahead, but it wasn't coming, so I gave it up. But I did get as far as outlining the book, and I now used that old outline as a framework. This time, the information just flowed. It was coming to me so quickly that it was difficult for me to write fast enough to keep up with it.

The book was literally given to me word for word. I had to balance my time between the clinic and writing, which meant putting in a full day at the clinic and then coming home and writing from ten until three, sometimes four o'clock in the morning. I would write a page, put it into its appropriate shoe box, then Joe would type it into the computer. This went on for weeks, until his work required that he work late hours, and he taught me how to use the computer. And as I wrote, and the book was unveiled, we knew that the book was coming to me—was given to me—almost by divine revelation.

Joe was concerned that after I had put so much energy into writing, I might not find a publisher. When he finally asked me what I would do, I told him the truth: "I don't know, honey, I was just told to write it. When I had the experience I was told then that it would be done, so I'm guessing that what that meant was that the book will be published." Aware of how much it meant to me to have this book published, Joe unselfishly offered the retirement money we had saved if we needed to publish it ourselves. I was moved by his concern and respect for what I felt called to do. But certain that God would guide me to the next step once I finished, I prayed, asking God if he would be very specific and let me know how this book was going to be published.

During a vision, I was told that the publisher would

seek me out, and that I would recognize the publisher by the "tones" in his voice, and this is what I told Joe and the other people who knew I was writing and were starting to ask. I knew that my answer was difficult for them to understand since I had no way to convince them, but they all waited to see. While in the spirit world I had learned about "tones" and how our spirit often recognizes another just by their tones, the music of their soul. This music can be sensed from the mortal body through its vibrational expression—our voice.

Soon, a publisher did call me. He had received a copy of the notes that were in circulation and wanted to include my story in a collection of stories about near-death experiences. I knew that the book he was describing was not the book I had been called to write. *Embraced*, I knew, was to stand on its own, but from his "tones" I thought he was the one that God had sent to me, and we reached an agreement for him to publish *Embraced by the Light* by itself. I had heard from other publishers and had turned them down, and I was glad that I did because this one *sounded* right.

I realized that I had made a mistake when another publisher called, also after reading the notes, and told me that he had a *passion* to publish the book. When he first began to speak on the phone, I "knew" him by the tones of his voice. I sat stunned by what I heard him say, and I reached for my journal and read, ". . . and you will know him by the tones of his voice—and he will say he has a *passion* to do this book!" I knew that I was now talking to the publisher God had told me about, and that the passion he mentioned was the other sign that God had given me. But it was too late, I had already signed a contract with the first publisher. Joe, noticing my reaction to this call, interrupted to see if everything was okay. I nodded, but the tears began to stream down my cheeks. "Why didn't you call a couple of weeks ago?" I blamed him. "I have been waiting for you to call!" "I called you as soon as I found your phone number," he answered— he had received a copy of the notes that did not contain my number—but he wasn't puzzled by my question to him. He was, however, anxious to see if he could get the rights from the other publisher. I told him that he was too late and gave him the name of the publisher who had bought the manuscript. As soon as I hung up the phone, I ran to be alone and wept. I cried because I had too loosely followed God's instructions. Had I paid more attention, I would have remembered that fateful word "passion."

Again, I prayed that God would forgive me and help this publisher to get the rights, and I promised to listen more carefully and more specifically the next time he gave me information.

It wasn't long before the first publisher told me that he couldn't publish my story "as is," requesting that I change it to reflect his own belief system. When I refused, he sold the manuscript to the publisher I knew was meant to publish it—Gold Leaf Press, which was first formed to publish *Embraced*. God had led me where I needed to be. But he wasn't finished yet.

About the time the book was to go out into the world, my publishers sent for me; we were scheduled to do some taping, and I'm sure they, too, were curious to meet in person the woman behind this manuscript. I stayed at the home of Curtis Taylor and his family and visited with the other people from the publishing company that night at his home.

We stayed up late, finally getting to bed just before one o'clock. I slept in the Taylors' daughter's bedroom and set the clock to be up at five. I had clients to see that afternoon, so I needed to catch the first morning flight home. Exhausted, I crawled into bed and drifted quickly to sleep, only to be awakened shortly afterward. The words I heard spoken softly were, "Open your eyes." The voice was familiar, but I had not heard it for some time. I opened my eyes, and standing there at the side of my bed were my three beloved friends whom I had not seen since my experience—the three guardian angels whom I fondly refer to as "the monks."

I was filled with joy to see them, and they radiated the love I had basked in before. I wanted to hold them and be held by them again. I also wanted to ask them where they had been all these years. They "knew" I had a lot of questions for them and that I wanted to share our love, but they told me instead that they had some information to give me. They were warm, but the moment was serious and I could sense that.

"Close your eyes and rest as we instruct you," one of them said. And I did, after glancing at the clock. I drifted off into what felt like sleep, unable to consciously remember what they communicated to me or how long the communication lasted. But I was awakened every hour on the hour by the three monks, who would immediately tell me to close my eyes again, and would communicate with me further. When they awoke me at four o'clock, I indicated that I was going to need their help if I was to get up at five. "You have kept me so busy that I have not had much sleep," I teased them.

I closed my eyes, and they continued to communicate with me, giving me information. They woke me again at 4:57, and when I looked at the clock, I said, "Hey, guys, I still have three more minutes, you've gotten me up too early." But they were gone before I could finish. I smiled, knowing they had heard me anyway. After I dressed and met Curtis in the kitchen, I told him what had happened, knowing that there must be a reason why they woke me when they did at 4:57. I asked him to check the accuracy of the clock.

It was no surprise to learn that the clock was three minutes off. I knew that these wonderful friends had, in their way, been joking with me, showing me that they would do as I asked, while pointing out that the clock was off. They were reminding me that they were there, but there, with me, in a stronger, more meaningful way than I might realize.

I didn't remember consciously what they expressed to me during that visit. But I felt encouraged that I had been given direction I would recognize when I needed it. I "knew," too, that they would be present in my moments of need as I faced the challenges ahead. And I "knew" that they were there to help me deliver *Embraced* to the world.

Visions Fulfilled

*N*ow that the book was out, I turned to God for guidance on how to get it to as many people as possible. He showed me that it would go out into the world in wave after wave, in ever larger circles, just like the ripple effect of good deeds I had seen in the spirit world.

I had kept in a notebook the names of those who had responded to the notes back when they were being circulated. The people who called me wanted me to contact them as soon as the book was published. Some offered to help in any way I needed. When I did need assistance in their particular area, not one person turned me down. Each person mentioned that they had a *passion* for the message, and shared with me some unusual stories about how they knew that they were supposed to help. God led me to the right people, and soon I was speaking several times a week to audiences of hundreds assembled on short notice by the people I had asked for help.

It was exciting, thrilling, to see everything that I was shown being unveiled. Each person I would have contact with would refer me to another person, who would refer me to yet another person. I was told that all the right people were going to be in position, ready to do their part. I just needed to make that contact, and they would know by their spirit that it was their turn to take that ripple one step farther. I was excited to meet each person, because I knew that each was the perfect person in the perfect place at the perfect time.

They didn't necessarily know the details that I knew about *Embraced*, and their spirits were not necessarily in tune to their purpose, but they acted on the energy that God gave them and they did their part. Many of these wonderful people don't know to this day what they truly did. I often wanted to tell them, "Do you really know what you're doing for God and for all his children?" What they did was to create a greater ripple effect of tremendous energy that's going to affect generations to come. There were times when some of those who helped would recognize my spirit, and we knew that we were connected. But usually they didn't, and I didn't press the issue. If God had not unveiled the purpose to them, it was not my role to do so.

I came to rely on the energy of these wonderful people as I forged ahead in the routine of getting the word out, wherever we traveled. Our regular daily schedule began with early morning media appearances and continued through two or three book signings, concluding with a nightly presentation that usually didn't end until eleven.

Although I had overcome a tremendous amount of my phobias, I still had them. I was unsure how I was going to respond in public, around strangers, and away from home. And because I knew that I represented my experience—that people could decide whether or not they would accept the message I offered based on whether or not they accepted me—it was important that I did everything right.

I noticed that God began to place in my life people who carried spiritual energy that could sustain me along the way. I had been shown during my experience that we draw energy from each other—some people we receive energy from and some draw energy from us—in a constant exchange. When I shared my experience, I was sharing my energy, often to the point where I would feel I had nothing left. But there was so much energy being generated—there was such *excitement* in each meeting room, all the time—that there would always be someone there to supply the energy I needed to continue, no matter how depleted I felt.

God puts these people in our paths when we need them. He wants us to draw on the powers of heaven, and if we are attuned, we will recognize when we have a chance to tap into the energy he has provided for us or to be of service when our energy can help accomplish his will. Our strength, like our good deeds, sets the ripple into motion. It is the sacred sharing of love that keeps us going.

This can happen anywhere, if we're open to it. I experienced a very memorable explosion of loving energy in a glassed-in radio studio inside a busy casino, during one of my first visits to Las Vegas soon after publication. I felt a little ridiculous talking about my experience in the middle of a casino, where we could watch people gambling and playing slot machines and paying us absolutely no attention.

I had prayed for the energy I needed to do the best I could, but the circumstances of the day seemed to work against me. Our host, Lou, didn't quite understand what a near-death experience was all about, but as I began to talk to him he became mesmerized by my voice and by my experience. I, however, was losing my energy, sharing something so very sacred and spiritual in what seemed to be an inappropriate setting. When my publishers, Curtis Taylor and Stan Zenk, joined Lou and me in the studio, they noticed that I was struggling just to get through this experience. Curtis immediately sat down on the chair beside me, and Stan stood directly behind him—the four of us taking up just about all of the room that was left in this tiny glassed-in space.

And I began to draw on their energy. At first, I wondered what was happening; then I remembered our natural ability to tap each other's energy fields, and I saw the energy ripple among us. There was an abundance of energy. By now we were taking phone calls, and as I became energized and the energy flowed over the airwaves and out to the audience, it started coming back to us from the callers. Soon, we were supercharged. The whole room was filled with this incredible energy. All the host could say was, "Oh, boy. Oh, boy. I don't know what's going on here, folks. But, oh, boy. Oh, boy. If you were here in this studio, oh, boy."

We sent it out, and it came back, and we kept it up as long as we could, staying on the radio way beyond the scheduled thirty minutes. The transformation was unforgettable—from struggling through a difficult situation to reaching the people who were there for me to reach. God uses whatever is available to us to answer our prayers.

As exhausting as they were, the weeks after *Embraced*'s publication were filled with answered prayers. God was my constant source, and I prayed all the time. I found the strength I needed; we always do when we are doing God's will. And God gave me inspiration; certain things that were given to me, like mile markers. I came to learn that just before I'd collapse, I would reach that marker and say to myself, "Yes, I'm this far along. Just some more to go, Betty." And then I'd have the strength to go on some more.

Those mile markers were sometimes astonishing. In November I had prayed that by Christmas *Embraced* would be the best-selling book in the region in which we were touring. That was asking a lot for one month. Yet by Christmas it happened. And then it just snowballed from there. The presentations were getting larger and larger, so large that we often had to turn people away.

One presentation in particular showed me how powerful the reception to the message of *Embraced* had already grown. We were running late when we hit bumper-to-bumper traffic on the freeway four exits away from our destination. Cars were pulled off on the side of the road, and people were jumping out and running down the freeway. At one point when we were stopped by the backup, I asked a woman who was walking hurriedly along the road what was going on. She told me, "We're going to hear this speaker at the auditorium." When I asked who the speaker was, she said, "Betty Eadie." And I said, "Oh, my gosh!" It had just dawned on me what was happening. I hadn't related the traffic jam to my speaking engagement at all. Then, knowing that I didn't want her to feel embarrassed when she saw me later, I stuck my hand out the window and introduced myself, and assured her that nothing was going to happen until I got there. She grabbed my hand and started shouting my name, and soon others came running toward our car.

We didn't want to be slowed down by having to greet each person individually, so we drove on until we finally got to the school with the auditorium. Police had been called in to deal with the traffic. Cars were parked all over the street, on lawns, everywhere. The newspaper the next day compared the bedlam to a scene at a rock concert. But for us, it was a considerable challenge getting to the school, and, once there, getting in. The auditorium was filled to capacity, but that didn't keep people from filling every other available space— hallways, bathrooms, wherever they could turn. The building was so packed that the fire and police departments were trying to get people to leave. I wasn't sure how I would get to the stage.

When I finally did go out on stage to speak, the impact of *Embraced*, its message and its hope, suddenly dawned on me. I felt so inadequate. I felt humbled in my spirit. Bringing *Embraced* into existence and getting it out there, I knew I was doing the work that God wanted me to do. And I was grateful for the people who were sacrificing and doing their part, and whose efforts kept me going.

But now I was faced with what this really meant. It was so much bigger than me. It didn't matter why it was me who was bringing this message. It wasn't happening just to me. It was happening to all of us.

I was thankful for the lights shining on me when I stepped out on stage because their brightness blinded my view beyond the first few rows. I don't know if I could have spoken to that group that night if I had seen its immensity. I shared my message as I had on previous nights, but I shared it with perhaps a little more strength, because I felt the spirit so strongly in these people.

They just wanted me to tell them more about Jesus. They wanted to hear about unconditional love. They wanted to hear that they are perfectly who they need to be, and that they are in the right place to advance in their walk with God. They wanted to feel God's love, as I had, and I was anxious to share it with them.

And as I spoke to this group of people, I knew that I could not have stood there in front of them to share any part of my experience, or any part of me, without knowing that God was there beside me. But I knew that he was there with me and would be there on my continuing journey, more than I had ever known before.

"David Stone"

*T*he telephone kept ringing, I was rushed for time, I had found a run in my new hose, a television crew was due at my house at any moment, and I was frantic. I remembered being asked during another interview what my life was like now that I was famous. *Well, if they could see me now!* I thought.

I always prepared early for interviews because I enjoyed a few minutes of solitude to collect my thoughts and some time to spend in prayer. It didn't look as if that would happen today.

The phone rang again. I let it ring, ignoring it for the third time, hoping someone else in the house would answer it.

"Mom, it's for you!" one of the kids hollered out. "It's a man, but he won't give his name. He sounds kind of funny."

One more thing that I had not thought about! Our phone number and address had been available to the public for the twenty-six years that we lived here. The phone rang constantly now that the book was out, the callers wishing me well or wanting to share their own near-death experiences or their grief. Although they were time-consuming, I really did not mind the phone calls. Most of the people calling respected my time or were willing to let me go when I told them I had something important to do or that I was in the middle of dinner.

I was just about to ask if someone would tell this man that I could not come to the phone, when intuition told me to take the call.

"Hello, this is Betty."

"Betty, thank you for taking my call. I know you must hear from hundreds of people like me . . . with problems."

The man's voice was firm and steady but contained a tone of tremendous sadness so strong I could feel it. I took a long deep breath to calm myself as I glanced once more at the clock, deciding that the run in my hose and the dust on the furniture wouldn't show up on television.

"We all have problems," I answered him. I tried to speak softly, with concern. "But it's the solutions to the problems that I most often worry about! How about you?"

"Solutions . . . yes, if there are any that will help," he continued, his voice showing no change in emotion. "I saw you on television, Betty, and I must confess that I have not read your book. I just needed someone that I could talk to today, someone who would just listen, and I thought of you. You had a tenderness in your voice when I heard you speak, and I could see from the look in your eyes that you really care about people. You are not a surface person, like most of the people I've met."

I could readily see that this phone call was going to take some time, the one thing that I had little of today. My attention was drawn in two separate directions, and I felt that I desperately needed to get off the phone for final preparations for the interview. Still, I was sensing that the caller was desperate, too.

"What's your name?" I asked, trying to fill in the space left by his long pause.

"My name is not important anymore. You see, this is the last day I will ever have on this earth. In fact, Betty, you are the last person that I will be talking to. I have made the decision to take my life. This has not been an easy decision; trust me, I have thought this out for a long, long time. Now, I did not call you for advice, nor do I want any. I only needed someone to say good-bye to. Someone I felt would care that I even existed! If you try to talk me out of my solution, I will have to say good-bye now and hang up."

I was pacing the floor while he talked, the phone receiver to my ear and its cradle in my other hand. The house was filling up fast, and the only empty, quiet room available to me now was the bathroom. I stretched the telephone cord out as far as it would allow me, but the phone's base couldn't reach through the bathroom door. Leaving the cradle in the hallway, I pulled the coiled cord of the receiver under the door as I shut it; now, sitting on the floor by the door, I finally had some privacy.

The man on the phone was absolutely serious about his intentions, and I felt totally helpless and unable to reach him.

"Listen, it sounds like you have everything figured out," I said to him boldly. "I can't imagine trying to talk you out of this either. I don't know anything about you. So, even if I did want to talk you out of taking your own life, which I don't, I really wouldn't know what to say to you anyway."

I held my breath. I was breathing way too fast, and I did not want him to sense my panic.

Slowly I moved to my knees on the floor. The single run in my stocking spread farther down and across my leg, but it didn't matter now—only one thing did. I was totally focused on this man and his problem. There was only one solution for me, and that was to pray to God for help, now!

"Father," I began to pray silently, urgently to myself. The energy inside me demanded much more of a release, but I knew that for the time being, I had to remain calm, even in this moment of prayer. I remembered the bright lights I had seen in the spirit world, as prayers of great need shot forcefully from the earth, and I held this vision in my thoughts as I prayed. "Father, this man is in immediate need of your divine intervention. I pray that your spirit will surround him now, and that you will show him another way to solve his problems. But let it be your will that is done, not . . ."

"Betty, are you still there?" his voice brought me suddenly back to him.

"Yes, I'm listening," I managed to respond. "Oh, Father!" I continued in silent prayer, "please be with me, and place in my mind the right words to say to . . ."

"I'm not interrupting anything, am I?" he politely continued. "I don't mean to bother you, really I don't."

His words were spoken smoothly, but at the same time they sounded cold and stony. I knew that this child of God had lost his awareness of the heavenly worth of every soul, had lost sight of the light of God in him; I felt he had a gun at his head and at any moment, if I said the wrong words, I would hear it go off.

"I'm fine here," I said, trying very hard to introduce

something positive. "Take your time; I really would like to get to know you."

I heard him take a deep breath followed by a sigh. There was so much that I wanted to ask him. I could see the darkness he was in. I thought of the despair I had lived through, and I knew how far out of reach hope can seem. But I also knew that we must try to reach it. Our despair is never justified. We must always seek hope; it was there for me, and it would be for this man, too. It was becoming difficult for me not to jump right in with questions, but I knew that right now was not the time to ask them.

My heart was pounding. My legs began to ache. I tried to reposition my body, but the telephone cord was pulled as far as it could go, leaving very little space for me to move in.

"Let me explain to you, Betty, that first I am an intelligent person, well educated, with a college degree. I have always believed in God and have been a member of my church all of my life. Both my parents and their parents have been devout members of the same church all of their lives. We are well known in our community and have always been active in it.

"As a young man, I became a missionary, then married my high-school sweetheart shortly after the mission. We were married in the church and were extremely active in all of our church duties. We had two children. I had a well-paying job, and in a very short time we accumulated material things that most people our age could not afford.

"My job began to require frequent absences away from home. In her loneliness, my wife began to see another man. Their relationship, as I came to understand it, was purely platonic. But I found that difficult to accept, so I began to see another woman. My wife left me and took the children with her. We had started to work things out when the most terrible thing happened. I committed adultery with the woman I was seeing! This ended it for my wife, and she got a divorce. My family turned against me and the only emotional resource I had left was the church.

"As my behavior became known, the church leaders asked me to leave the church and I was excommunicated. In my despair I turned to drink . . . and worse still, to another woman.

"My employers and most of my associates at my job are also members of my church and were well aware of my promiscuous behavior and, because of that, continued advancement in my job became impossible. When it became necessary to lay off employees, I was one of the first to go.

"After spending some time in counseling, I began a turnaround. I quit drinking, broke off my relationships with other women, and began attending church with the desire to reinstate myself. I visited my children often, and things began to look better between my ex-wife and me. Or so I thought. A couple of weeks ago, she informed me that she and the man she was seeing intend to be married!"

As he continued pouring out his heart to me, I began to tune in to his despair, my spirit matching the frequency of his spirit, to the point that I was literally at his level of understanding and could feel all his pain and emotions. This gift of discernment was given to me before my return to earth, and it was often unsettling to my spirit. When I connected with someone, it wasn't always by conscious choice, and the attunement was often quite painful. This time was no exception.

"I'm not looking for your sympathy," he solemnly stated. "Not even your understanding. I just needed to tell someone, just needed to talk. I thank you for being there for me, even if it is on the other side of this telephone line." Once more, I could hear a sigh. It was not a sigh of release, however, but rather, a sigh of resignation, and that troubled me. It reminded me of the resignation I had felt. I knew how hard it can be to find the way back to God, and I knew it was up to this man to do so.

"Will you at least tell me your first name? I like to address people by name when I talk to them." I needed to stall for more time . . . for what, I didn't know. But I felt that I had to keep him busy talking or listening.

"Betty, you are a great listener. I'm glad that I had the

chance to explain myself. My mind was made up when I called. I have nothing left to live for."

"You have your children! How can you forget them?"

"She has them, and has turned them against me, too."

"If I were in your shoes, I don't believe I would take my life—but then I'm not you, and you are in control of your own destiny." I spoke with confidence, even though I felt little of it at the time.

"I heard you out, now could I at least speak my mind—about what I think of your dilemma?" I continued.

"It probably is only fair, but I warned you, you will not change my mind."

I filled my spirit with love for this man I couldn't see, whose name I didn't know, and opened my heart to him. "Okay then, let me tell you what I learned about suicide and why I think it is not an alternative to living and working out the solution."

I could hear him breathing quietly, and I knew that he was still on the phone, but he said nothing. His silence made me believe that I had not won any battles. I felt, however, that no matter how troubled this man had become, he still believed in God, and loved him. His spirit still held some measure of the God-given desire to do good—to love—and I could sense that however dim it might have gotten, the light of God's love was still shining in him. Knowing this, I had the advantage that I needed, and now was the time to use it.

"We must never consider suicide," I stated flatly, taking a chance that he would listen. I was feeling a bit shaky but knew that I needed to continue speaking confidently. "God loves all of us, and that includes you. We are here on earth to grow, spiritually, by using our free will to create the actions that determine the course of our lives. If we stop our spiritual growth, we are violating the laws that govern us all. Taking our own life will cause us to lose opportunities that are needed to develop spiritually while we are on earth." I tried to bring him back into the conversation. "Do you believe in an afterlife?" I asked him.

"Yes, I guess so. But I don't know, Betty, I have lost hope in everything . . . everybody. Where is God when I need him? Back then! Now?" The pitch in his voice was higher now than it had been before, and that made me nervous. I did not want him to become annoyed and hang up on me.

"Can I tell you a little about what happened to me and why I wrote *Embraced by the Light*?" I asked him. He was silent again. I took that for a sign of either acceptance or acquiescence. I gave him a brief account of my near-death experience: first my death, the tunnel, meeting Jesus, and finally the part that I was most anxious to share with him, the life review of the ripple effect that we create.

"After the death of our body, we have a life's review where we experience the ripple effect of our creativity—

or the lack of it for that matter," I told him. "We don't just watch our lives. We *experience* the effects that our actions have had on others. It can be a painful experience; no one wants the mistakes of their actions brought before them in a place of such purity and love. But the life review is an important part of our spiritual growth. And when you have been brought back in touch with the love you carry within you, and you feel the results of your mortal actions, you will judge yourself in a way that you may not think is possible here on earth."

I paused for a moment before proceeding. "You still carry that love in you today, and you are here to share it with others. You still have the opportunity to do so. Suicide creates a great vacuum of lost opportunities, a vacuum that can be filled with pain and sorrow. God, though, is the judge of each of our lives, and only he really knows the depth of each soul's trials. We are here to learn, to experience life by using our free will. You can still use your free will to change your heart, forgive yourself, and move back to God. You have made mistakes, but you can still feel his love. They don't see sin in the spirit world as we do. God knew we would make mistakes. Life is all about mistakes. It is constant change and growth. Our greatest challenges in life will one day be known to us as our greatest teacher."

"I never asked for this, Betty. And I cannot imagine what I could possibly learn from all this pain. I want it to go away! You have got to understand, this is the only way that I see it."

"Well, I don't see it that way," I responded. "Suicide is a temporary fix; you leave your misery only for a brief moment until you meet it again face-to-face in your life review. You interrupt your spiritual development, the growth that determines your experience in heaven. We are all at different levels spiritually—here and there. If you don't develop here, you will have to do so there. The wonders of heaven are beyond our comprehension—if we live true to the spirit we came to earth with, we can progress more quickly. We do that by expressing the love of God that is within us, and we do that by loving God, ourselves, and each other. It is that simple. I'm sorry that you hurt, and I wish with all my heart that I could share some of your pain. But you can find the love you need. God is always with us, he is constant. He is like the sun and we are like the earth. We revolve around him. He never moves away from us, but often we move from him."

A sharp tap at the door startled me. "Mother, are you all right in there?" I could hear concern in my daughter Donna's voice. "The makeup person is waiting. Can I help you do anything?" I covered the mouthpiece on the phone and whispered to her that I was fine and would be out soon.

"I'm sorry." His voice too was lowered to a whisper. "I have kept you far too long."

"Wait a minute," I whispered back. Knowing that Donna was still standing outside the door and eager to keep our conversation private, I cupped my mouth to the phone. "I haven't finished. There is more that I want to tell you!"

"I need to go. Thank you for your time, and I'm sorry if . . ."

"You need to understand something!" I shouted back at him.

"Mother . . ."

"Look," I continued, "the legacy you leave behind for your children goes on." My voice was calmer now, but firm. "The decisions you make and your actions affect your children's lives. Through them it will ripple out to their children and then to their children's children and more, for generations. If you open your heart to God's love today and share that love in your actions, you will feel its beauty when your spirit reaches God. But if you take your life, pain, shame, fear, and guilt will be your gift not only to your children but to your parents and other family members as well. The ripple effect of what you are about to do, and how it affects each person that you are connected to, will also be experienced by you. Believe me, I am not your judge, but I believe that suicide is a selfish act, and I know that you are not a selfish man. You are in God's hands. He is your judge."

"Mother, are you okay?" Donna was becoming more

concerned, and I couldn't blame her. I must have been in the bathroom for a long time. But time meant nothing to me now, and I did not feel free to respond to her. My body was beginning to tremble from the position I had been forced to hold for what now seemed to me like forever.

"Thank you, Betty, I have to go." The coolness in his voice was indication enough for me that his heart was hardened and set. He had every intention to follow through with his plan to end his life. "I told you from the beginning that I had thought this out carefully," he continued, "and I would not have bothered you, but I knew that you would care. I love you, Betty. Don't blame yourself for what I am about to do."

"I won't," I said. I reached for a towel that was hanging just above my head and held it to my eyes. My tears were hot against my cheeks and my throat tightened as I squeezed out my final words to him. "I don't even know your name, but I love you, too."

I heard him hang up the phone. I guess there was no reason to say good-bye. Tears blinded my eyes, but I didn't have time for that now. I opened the door and shouted at Donna to get the telephone book. I had numbers for two churches that had hot lines for prayer. I had used them before because I knew that the power of prayer, when used in unity with others, was the most powerful weapon man has.

Donna found the numbers for me and dialed one. A soft voice answered and asked for my request. "For whom would you like us to pray?"

"Well," I stammered, "I, ah, well, I . . . don't know." Immediately I silently prayed for God to help me give him a name. "He's David," I said quickly. King David of the Bible had popped into my mind. He believed in God and yet fell away. He, too, had committed adultery, much like my new friend.

"A last name?" she asked.

"Stone," I hastily replied. "Yes, David Stone."

I had chosen *Stone* for "David's" last name because his heart was hardened and he had no vision of his future. A miracle was needed, and I knew that if it was the will of God and not David's time, intervention would change the course that destiny now offered. I know that God loved us so much that he gave us free will—even if that meant that we might take our own life, breaking a spiritual law that we all agreed upon before coming to earth.

I hung up the phone. It seemed an eternity had passed since I first picked it up. The camera crew was patiently waiting; it had taken them some time to set everything in the right place for the proper lighting. I sat, and the makeup artist began her job. My red, swollen face meant nothing to her but a challenge. The reporter moved forward and sat down next to me.

"Betty, do you mind if I ask you a few of the questions

now, before we are taped, to give you some time to think them over beforehand?" When I gave no response, she continued, "What I'd like to ask is, how has the book changed your life?" She smiled warmly, unaware of what I was going through. "And, second," she continued, smiling, "besides us intruding on you, what other exciting things have happened to change your lifestyle now that you are famous?"

Tears stung my eyes again. My thoughts were elsewhere—with "David Stone." But I knew the responsibility for God's message of love was the more important concern in my life, and I knew that it would be that way forever.

"I'm sorry, Ms. Eadie, did some of the makeup get into your eyes?"

"Yes," I replied. "Yes, I think it did."

Family Concerns

Embraced was published in November, so it seemed the natural Christmas gift for my extended family and Joe's. The response was not entirely as I had imagined or hoped for. Although by now most of them had known of my experience, and I had already talked to them about the message I felt compelled to share in my book, some of them were very uncomfortable with the subject matter, particularly Joe's brother, Tom—a professed atheist.

Over the years, Tom had often sat across the table from me and we had discussed in great detail the information that I received during my experience. He found the information about God and God's great love for us was very interesting, but he didn't have a belief in God. In fact, he felt the God he had learned about in his childhood didn't exist for any of us and that everything is lost at the moment of death. "When you die," Tom would say, "you are just gone."

We could get into some heavy debates over this, although our great respect and love for each other kept us from the point of argument. It got to be a regular pattern in our friendship; every time he'd come over, we'd get back on the same subject of my belief and his lack of it. The fact that I had finally managed to put my experience into a book, and that the book was bringing its message to an ever-expanding group of people, did nothing to sway his position.

Still, I wished I had been able to get through to him. A person as wonderful and loving as Tom, no matter how much he had internalized God-like qualities, was inevitably held back by his lack of belief and faith in God. There are plenty of atheists who live as true or even more true to God's attributes than many religious people do, but they are missing something by leaving God out of their lives. If you can see ahead and you know that death does not end in the grave, you actually do a little more preparation and challenge yourself more. Knowing that you are responsible for your deeds and knowing of the ripple effect that they all set into motion, you spend more time preparing for the other side instead of just preparing for death.

People who die as nonbelievers can eventually see God. He loves us so much that even after death he won't force us out of one belief system into another without choice. As I journeyed in the black space before the light, I saw many people who remained after I left. I knew that they didn't know the love of God, even though God loved them. He was keeping them there, bathing them with love until they reached the point that they knew of his existence and could move on to another level.

I saw the gift of free will at work in Tom's decision to maintain his opinion in spite of everything I said and everything that had started to happen with *Embraced*. He was a reminder to me of the urgency of the work I was doing. My immediate family—my husband, kids, and grandchildren—gave me another reminder of the sacrifices I would need to make to continue my service.

I hadn't quite internalized my role in all of this. It was being given to me bit by bit, as God wanted me to have it. As I was writing the book, I had started to think about the responsibility of it. But I had never thought about the publishing effort, never heard of a book tour, and never been to a book signing. What I thought about, instead, was the sharing of my life with others, because I had always been a private person.

After the first tour, I suddenly realized what my sacrifice was going to be. I would have to change my current lifestyle with my family, and we were very close. Little Betty was thirteen, so I didn't have small children at home. But being a protective mother, I didn't want to be far from my children, even though the rest were adults. I also wanted to be there for my grandchildren, to be home for my kids. But when I realized that wasn't going to happen very often, I knew then why God had allowed me to go and see my children when I left the hospital in spirit. I had seen then that they would be fine without me. They were not my mission. It confirmed my faith that I had another purpose and that it was now time for me to proceed with that. My children were actually happy for me and very supportive. I had been told to surround myself with the people who loved me the most, and I knew that those in my family were the right people.

In the spirit world, I received pure knowledge of Satan's desire to destroy the family. I was shown that he is trying to do that by reaching the women first, as he had done before. When God created the different roles for men and women, he kept women close to himself in spirituality, as co-creators of life, and it is inherent in the female to take greater spiritual risks than the male to accomplish this. I was shown that Eve made this choice when she chose mortality in order to bear children. Satan fears the spirituality in women and God's need for them to be the nurturers of children. He attempts to access the next generation by removing both spirituality and the mother from the home. By destroying the family unity, the bond, he can feel confident of success.

I was shown very clearly that a void is created in our

homes when mothers leave their children, particularly during the crucial years in which the child bonds with the mother, the giver of life. The first three years of life is the time when the child learns the most intimate bond of life, the bond with love—love of self, which the mother's love provides, and the love of family, which prepares them for society. The ripple effect of pain produced by the lack of a family bond, especially when the mother is not in the home, is carried through into adulthood. The child, not bonding, can turn against parent, and parent, not having bonded, can turn against child.

The ripple effect of life begins here, in our homes, with our chosen families, and I taught my children accordingly. No service anywhere else is more important to us, to them, or to the world. I was shown that the strength of the family is the strength of the world; to destroy that would be to destroy us all. I was also shown that charity begins in the home, and that each family group must first take care of its own. I understood that it was to begin in the home, then ripple out to others. I was also shown that we must all be careful not to do too much for others, which can enslave them by taking away their self-worth. Destroying self-worth would disable them and then destroy generations of that same family group. Each ripple eventually connects, one with the other, until we are united as one, and we are all responsible for each other. I understood, too, that when this life's experience was over, we could return to our beginnings in heaven and continue as a family there as well, if we so chose. I saw that the spirits of family members can also be among those who greet us when we do return to the spirit world.

With my kids all beyond that crucial age, I knew my call to share my life and my message outside of the home had come. I knew, too, that many women in the world like me, grandmothers, were in the process of fighting back against Satan. I was shown the awakening of women to the perils that they face and the reawakening of mothers and grandmothers everywhere to the special purpose of all mothers to protect the family and return it to the strong, nurturing unit in which children can learn to love.

My concerns for my family and the impact of my new life on them were typical of the balance of worldly and spiritual issues that I now needed to maintain. When I first returned to my flesh, I was so filled with the spirit that it was difficult for me to live in the flesh as a human being. I had to change that and become more spiritually balanced—not too spiritual, but mortal as well, "so that my feet would touch the ground," as Joe would put it.

During my experience, I learned that there are two parts to every person. They can be described in various ways: male and female, intellectual and emotional, protective and nurturing, right brain and left brain. Often here on earth we go through life being one way or the other, but we can learn to balance both parts. In fact, being off balance, too far one way or the other, is an abuse—a gluttony of the spirit—that keeps the spirit away from where it needs to be to achieve its greatest growth.

To maintain my effort, I needed to always seek the appropriate balance, and after my experience, I began to see that happening. I returned with the male side of my personality more pronounced in my presence; I felt more confident, desired fewer boundaries, and my handshake even changed. The change in balance that took place as I ventured farther out into the world had obvious effects on my family. I was no longer the full-time nurturing mother I had been, and they had to adapt to that.

But when a spirit is in balance, it is at its greatest strength. I needed all the strength I could summon to continue on my journey. In letting go of the balance I had struck for years in my family to fulfill that, I had to struggle to find a new balance. And for that, I needed my faith in God and in my belief I was doing the right thing. Up to this point, I could see that God was always moving me in the right direction; whenever I'd step off, he would gently guide me back, always putting me in a position where my faith would have to be tested. And it is in the testing of our faith that we can experience the greatest growth. He tested me in areas that were most challenging, and I had to make some very tough decisions based upon the challenge, sometimes on a moment's notice. And the more I was challenged, the stronger I became in my belief that the message was of utmost importance for everyone. As bearer of it, I was willing to make the sacrifices necessary—both those I knew of and those still to come.

Another Special Angel

God not only prepares us to do his will, he also gives us all that we need to do it. He sends to our path the right people when we need them, whether we realize it or not. Our spiritual attunement to God helps us to recognize the spirits sent to us, even if the reason for them being there is not immediately apparent. One day, soon after *Embraced* was published, my path was crossed by a young girl whose spirit restored my faith in my work at a time when I sorely needed it.

It was midday, and I was signing books after two intense weeks of interviews, signings, and speaking engagements that had been physically exhausting. The effort was literally making me sick; I had learned earlier

132

that day at a doctor's office that I was having an allergic reaction to the paper the book was printed on. A few weeks earlier, my three-year-old grandson, Zach, had hit a grand slam straight to my nose, fracturing it in several places. When I postponed surgery to make this trip, my doctor warned me about sinus infections; now I learned I had a severe one. I was also discouraged by some of the negative remarks at the presentation the night before, a feeling made worse by my absence from home and loved ones. I knew that I was doing as God wanted me to, I just had not expected what would be required of me when I did it.

I signed books as rapidly as I could, hoping to finish during the allotted time. The physical pain I felt left me unprepared to deal with the emotional pain that I encountered so frequently at these events. Many people came to me with their spirits lifted, rejoicing in the message that I shared, and my spirit would soar with theirs. But many came in the pain of grief and loss, and I could feel it again and again in my soul.

As the line of people waiting for their books to be signed wound around the perimeter of the bookstore, my attention was drawn to the entrance, where in rushed a woman with an angelic little girl. As I continued to sign books, I occasionally glanced up to see where the child stood in the line. I was curious about her. This was a school day, and my maternal instincts immediately caused me to question why she wasn't in school. I supposed this was why I was wondering about her. It was not long before they stood before me. The first words out of my mouth voiced the thoughts I had had from the moment I laid eyes on her. "Why aren't you in school, honey?" I asked, then without waiting for an answer, "Are you out for vacation or sick?"

Little Betty had been on my mind earlier. In my homesickness, I had thought about how she was doing in school. Had I not been so distracted by those concerns, I might have noticed that there was something different about this child. Looking at her now, I could clearly see that her eyes were swollen from tears. Reaching for her hand I looked at her mother; an identical pair of swollen, tearstained eyes stared back at me. There was no response to my inquiry, as both mother and daughter struggled to compose themselves.

"This is Holly," the mother finally said, gently guiding the child toward me. "Holly is eight years old. She has been ill for the past couple of years and has just had her third heart operation." As she continued to speak, I acknowledged what she was saying with little nods of my head. "Holly hasn't been in school for a while, and because she was home I was able to read her your book. She saw you on TV and heard you would be signing your book here today. Holly pleaded with me to bring her to you because she has something important to tell you."

Holly's mother bent down close to her weeping daughter and stroked the golden curls that framed her sweet little face. I glanced again at the child . . . her eyes so mature, yet innocent. Holly, sensing my love for her, moved closer to me, and I squeezed her hand, sharing my strength with her.

Slowly and deliberately she spoke between sobs. "You see, Betty," she said, "I saw Jesus, too, like you said you did in your book. When I had my last surgery, I died like you did. Jesus came and met me. He hugged me, too."

Her body began to tremble as she cried, and I wanted so badly to pull her into my arms. Her mother was racked in grief from listening to her brave little girl, but we both knew Holly wasn't finished with what she had come to tell me, so we didn't move or interrupt her.

"He . . ." she began again, stuttering ever so slightly, "he, well, he told me that it was time for me to come home now." Her throat tightened and a high-pitched sound came from her voice as she continued speaking. "I want to go home where he is, but it makes my mommy and daddy sad. You see, I'm the only girl, but I have two brothers. When I'm gone, my mommy and daddy will have no daughter at home."

I knew now why Holly's eyes had looked both mature and innocent to me. The windows to her soul had opened to me, and I had no doubt that she had died and had seen Jesus. I understood completely her desire to go back to be with him, but understood, too, her concern that leaving would cause pain for her family.

The wisdom of understanding and concern for her

family was strong in Holly. Her knowledge of God's love was evident, too, because she expressed that same love for her family . . . unconditional love. Her concerns were not for herself, but for them.

Because children who have near-death experiences are not bound to the strong belief systems that hinder many adults, they are more open and accepting to the wonders of heaven and of God. I had heard from many of these children, and I knew that their experiences made a profound change in their lives. I remembered my first experience with death at the age of four and the difference it had made in my young life. After the doctors had pulled the sheets over my face and said that they had lost me, I saw a brilliant man with a beautiful white glistening beard. I loved him and I could feel his love for me. I remember thinking a lot about this man afterward, wondering who he was. I asked my parents often who they thought this man might be, but they never had an answer for me. They had not seen him. Throughout my life I was in search of the love that this beautiful man had shared with me. I believed in my heart that he was God.

My search for God continued to run deep within me throughout my childhood. At the Brainard Indian School, I sought out a secret place, which became sacred to me. It was on top of the mountain behind the girls' dormitory. I spent many afternoons there alone, looking down at the school nestled in the valley below, surrounded by mountains on three sides. The natural beauty of the woods and the majestic sunsets made me feel God's presence. I built an altar out of rock at the edge of the mountain, and I would kneel and offer my prayers of thanks to God for all the beauty I saw below and beyond me. I remember that it was never important to me whether he actually heard my prayers, I was just grateful for the chance to express my love for his creations.

Feeling the tightness of my jaw, I suddenly realized that my teeth were tightly clenched. Those remembered times had brought some relief from what I was experiencing now, but the sobs and tears of the two before me told me that this was only the beginning of an ocean of tears to be experienced later by them.

Holly turned and wrapped her little arms around her mother's neck, more to comfort her than to support herself. Her mother began to explain that Holly had been born with a heart defect that the doctors had not found until recently. Moving gently away from her mother, Holly turned back to me, this time reaching for my hand.

"Betty, Jesus told me that he hid my heart problem from the doctors because if they would have found it, they could have fixed it and I'm supposed to be going home soon." I marveled at this little girl's courage. Her bottom lip quivered, but there was a set look in her eyes and a firmness to her jaw that conveyed great strength and wisdom.

I thought of the spirits I had seen preparing to come to

earth and was reminded that all of their deaths were planned . . . as are all of ours . . . before we came. I knew some came knowing that they would be here for a short time. They were spirits who did not need long mortal lives to develop further spiritually but who chose to help the growth of the spirits of those they touched during their brief time on earth. I knew that the pain that their deaths left behind would be washed away when we are all reunited as spirits and that the suffering of those who remained longer was all part of the spiritual development that brings all of us here. We are here for the growth of the spirit, and as I looked into Holly's eyes, I felt both her family's pain and the power of her love, of the loving sacrifice of her purpose here on earth. Seeing the pure beauty of this child's soul touched my heart and filled me with love.

"Is there anything I can do?" I whispered, hoping that I could be of service to them.

"No, not really, thank you," the mother replied, "but there's more that Holly wants to tell you."

Holly's lips began to quiver again, and her eyes filled with tears as she stepped to my side to whisper in my left ear. "I talked to Jesus, Betty. He told me to tell you not to quit what you are doing!" Again her voice tightened to a squeak, and she repeated herself. "Don't ever quit, Betty!"

I couldn't restrain myself any longer. I reached and drew Holly into my arms and held her there. Tears and sobs could be heard from the three of us, but we were in our own world for now and felt unashamed.

"Holly, when you go back home to Jesus, will you give him a message for me," I asked. I could hardly speak, my voice was so filled with emotion. "Tell him that I love him and I won't quit, but I miss him so much!"

When Holly and her mother left the store, the concerns that had preoccupied me just a short while ago seemed less important now. I knew that the promise that I made before coming back to earth was one that I would always keep. The discomfort that I felt was nothing compared to the pain I knew was felt by not only this family but millions of others. By continuing to share the message of my experience, I knew they might find comfort and hope. No, I'll not quit; nothing else is as important to me.

This meeting happened over three years ago. I haven't heard from Holly or her parents, and I neglected to get an address. But Holly is always in my heart and in my thoughts as a special messenger from God. While I am in this mortal state, I will always miss the time I spent with Jesus. But quit? No, I haven't quit, not until my mission is complete.

A Piece of My Heart

The night after I returned home from my first tour, an unusual messenger visited me, appearing in his spirit. He spoke to me using a language that I recognized as Lakota Sioux, my native tongue. Although I had not used this language as a child, I had heard it spoken before. Other than a couple of derogatory words I remember often being used at the Indian schools by the students, I would not have been able to understand this language if it had been spoken to me under any other circumstance. We had not been allowed to speak in our native tongue, and my family, being half white, did not use the language at home. It was clear to me that I was intended to understand the message I was given; as the messenger spoke it in spirit, and I understood him completely.

"Betty, you are in your awakening," he said. I couldn't see his face or his body, but his presence was one of great strength. He represented himself as a Native American. I felt that he was somehow a part of me or perhaps of my purpose; the nature of the connection wasn't clear, but the power of the bond between us was.

"And, as a part of your awakening and your protection," he continued, "you will need to wear your native dress." This was said to me as though I owned and was accustomed to wearing such clothing. I responded that I didn't own anything like that and I didn't know where to get such a dress, thinking, too, that I'd be the last person to wear it if I did. I had not been involved in my native culture and would have a hard time explaining my sudden change of heart. I wanted to argue these points, but the messenger was gone as quickly as he had arrived.

My book was selling rapidly, and I felt a responsibility to it. The message I was given to share in *Embraced* was as sacred as it was urgent to me. It was important that I avoid doing or saying anything that could be used to discredit that message—which is what I thought critics and naysayers would try to do if I started to wear a native dress.

I immediately prayed about it and prayed again, because this was something that I was reluctant to involve myself with. I received no direct answer back, but I didn't expect one; I had come to realize that God would give me all I needed when it was time, and I had to trust that. Now I simply needed to do my part: to walk by faith. Without mentioning this to anyone, for fear of what their thoughts on the subject might be, I waited until the Lord sent me further guidance.

I didn't have to wait long. A few days later, a niece called to tell me she had found someone to make me a native dress. When she asked me if I wanted one, the question so surprised and excited me that I shouted, "Yes!" I felt this would be next. God had let me know that he would prepare the way if I were willing to follow.

Then a day or two later I received a call from a woman who told me, "Betty, you don't know who I am, but the Creator has told me something about you, and I thought you should know it." All of my senses sharpened as I listened to her continue. "You are in your awakening," she said. "God has great plans for you. He wanted you to hear this from an outside source."

By now I had heard about "the awakening" from several different people and in so many different ways that I became nervous about my reluctance to act on the message about the dress with enthusiasm. I made a promise to God that I would be more trusting in everything that I did for his purpose, whether it made sense to me or not.

The next call came from the woman who wanted to

make my dress. She sent me a drawing of what she had envisioned for me, and I knew immediately that this was the dress that the Lord wanted me to wear. In the garden of the spirit world, I had seen a glimmer of its grander joy, which I would never forget—a rose of breathtaking beauty, singing praise to the Lord with its own sweet tones. I experienced it when I entered it and became part of it, rejoicing as it grew because of me and my love for it. Now, embroidered with beads on each shoulder of the dress, were magnificent roses that immediately reminded me of that glorious rose I had experienced in the beautiful garden in the spirit world.

The rose has always had special meaning to me. Though its significance is still unknown to me, I know I will understand it at another time. When I was a child, the principal at Brainard Indian School named me Prairie Rose. And after my near-death experience, a shaman gave me the name Onjinjinkta, meaning, a rose that is red, ripe and blooming.

Remembering that the native dress was to be part of my protection, I wondered what that meant. Then, before my dress was completed, I read two articles that criticized the clothing that I had worn at my speaking engagements. I realized that the reporters were sensationalizing their reports, and the thought of my native dress began to bother me.

When the dress arrived, before I took it out of the

package, I stood looking at the open box. I walked around the table where I had placed it and continued to circle it, often walking away from it. The emotions that I began to feel about the dress disturbed me. I felt that this dress was more than protection, that there was a deeper purpose, and I knew that once I touched it, I'd be committed to that purpose.

Finally I lifted the dress from the box and held it to me, and as it touched my skin, I knew that it was a part of me . . . my spirit. And I knew in that moment that this is who I really am. I felt my cells rejoice. This feeling ran though me completely; it was indescribably wonderful! The doeskin dress was filled with an energy that lifted me spiritually! It had purpose, and that purpose was in my cells, eager to begin.

Joe wasn't sure what to think of my new image. He had gotten somewhat used to his unusual "new" wife, but he, too, had come to trust that I was honestly following in the directions that I thought God was leading me. Joe had personally witnessed the writing of *Embraced* and had watched what he said "was a miracle happen right before my eyes." Too many miracles had happened in our lives for him to question them now. It wasn't always easy for him to understand or to accept all of it, but he knew it wasn't easy for me either. Joe is an unusual man, having blind faith in a God and in an experience that he had never encountered.

The first time I wore my dress in public I was in New

York. When I walked out on stage, I felt great feelings of pride for my native heritage. I was filled with respect and honor for my people and what they represented. I began to "know" more about their awakening and what they shall become as they awaken. I noticed when I entered the room for the presentation, that there was a hush, a silence. I could sense respect and love coming to me from the audience. I knew at once that the dress captured their hearts, and then I understood a part of the protection. I knew that their spirits could remember things they had forgotten. Their connection to the Creator and the presence of the dress reminded them of the spiritual respect for one another that existed once before and that we should have again.

A deliberate flaw is left in everything that Native Americans make. They leave them as reminders that nothing created by man can be perfect, because only the Creator is perfect. On my dress is a little hand-stitched patch; every now and then, when I start feeling a little too much pride in my accomplishments, I slide my hand down the side of the dress and find the stitches that remind me that I am nothing without God, and only he is perfect.

Praise for me and my accomplishments was something that many people shared with me as my book had changed their lives. After presentations they would often come to me for an embrace, and their whispers of praise were often told into my silenced right ear . . . whispers I never heard. I would respond with a hug or a smile or any simple expression of God's love.

The protection from my native dress was painfully put to a test a few months later, when I met with one of the greatest challenges I have ever faced in my efforts to share the message of *Embraced*. My youngest son, Tom, and I arrived slightly late for a speaking engagement in a large city. The stadium was surrounded by a crowd when we pulled up and parked near the front stairs. I noticed that many of the people on the steps were carrying signs, some reading, "Betty Eadie Go Home," and others, "What Jesus Does Betty Believe In?" I could understand the "Betty Eadie Go Home" signs; obviously the message I had to offer in *Embraced* had made them feel uncomfortable, threatened. What I could not understand was, "What Jesus Does Betty Believe In?" I always believed that there was only one Jesus, as there is only one God, and I thought I had made that quite clear.

Tom asked me to stay in the car while he checked everything out, but there were police officers at the car as soon as he opened the door. "Ms. Eadie, we think you should go around to the back entrance," one of them said. "There are some protesters here, and we don't want you to get hurt." By now the protesters were chanting rude remarks. I felt protective of my son Tom, as he did me, but I wasn't going to be cowed by their signs.

"No, I won't go through the back door," I replied firmly. "I have never entered through the back door of any building because I had to, and I'm not going to start now."

As I lifted the long fringe of my dress to get out of the car, the feel of the garment sent a reminder to me that I was being protected now. God had given me the protection of the dome of light that shielded me after my return, when the demons had attempted their attack. I was told that Satan was angry that I had chosen to come back, and he had wanted to take my life then. I was protected from that challenge, and I had confidence now that God's protective love was still with me. The policemen moved in front as I left the car, and my son walked close behind me.

Then I saw other signs that disturbed me—anti-abortion signs. I wondered what this had to do with me. I had written in *Embraced* that abortion was something a woman should consider before doing. I shared with my readers the story about my decision not to abort my son Tom, the son who was with me now. I have never been pro-abortion but rather, pro-education on the facts that surround abortion. Many women are suffering because of this practice, often not fully understanding what abortion entails until after they have made the decision. They deserve to know the facts, both physical and spiritual. Many women have sought me out and told me about their agony over having aborted a child years before. What had seemed an answer to an immediate problem had only multiplied their sorrow later. I've met many a woman who would give all that she has for that one "lost" child. My heart goes out to those women; they are ours to love, not ours to judge.

During my time spent in the spirit world, I watched the wonderful delight with which spirits prepared to enter the bodies of their mortal mothers. Their mothers were special to them for many reasons. They were bonded spirits, friends, who were excited to come together once again with that loved one. Life on this earth as a mortal being is a necessary part of our spiritual development, and a woman giving of herself to another . . . giving life to her child . . . is of priceless worth to our Heavenly Father. I also knew that a bonded soul aborted in ignorance could choose to come back to that same mother as another child, an adopted child or even a grandchild. I was also shown that when a pregnancy resulted from incest or rape, the greater pain would be to continue with the child and that woman might have little choice.

As I walked slowly up the stairs toward the front door, my eyes began to look into the eyes of the many people who pushed toward me, shouting still: "Betty Eadie, go home, Betty Eadie, go home! What Jesus do you worship, Betty!"

Then, another moment happened when everything stood still. It's in that moment, when the spirit is quickened and its vibration exceeds that of all else, that everyone and everything stops; there is no sound, no movement. It happened to me now; no one spoke or moved. I could look at each person separately. I was looking for understanding, wanting to know what had caused them so much pain and bitterness.

Shortly after my experience, I had prayed for the removal of my ability to know the thoughts and feelings of people. I was told that I could grow into that "knowing" when I desired. All I had to do was focus on what I needed to know; if it was the will of the Father, I would know. I needed that "knowing" now to be of whatever help I could.

As I looked into those faces, I "knew" everything I needed to about why they were here now. I saw pain and fears that had been instilled in them, as they had been in me. These people had come because I had touched a very sensitive area in them, an area that was filled with fear created by the uncertainty of their own beliefs. I could tell that most of them had not read my book and that they were afraid to. The notion of God being everyone's God frightened them, and his *unconditional* love made them uncomfortable. I sent to each of their spirits a message of love from my heart, and I knew that they received it.

Instead of reacting to the protesters in a negative way, which would have been easy for me to have done before, I lowered my head and whispered "Macooa," meaning "a piece of my heart." It didn't matter whether they had heard me or not; my feelings of love for them were strong in me. God had heard my silent prayer of thanks; my dress had indeed been a protection for me. It had protected me . . . from myself.

I think that I was born with a sharp and fiery tongue. When I wanted to cut anyone with quick retorts, I did, and it often hurt them. My four brothers had taught me the surest ways to defend myself, and I had used those tools of defense to get even. My response to the angry protesters surprised me now. I definitely "knew" that my cells were awakening to God's wisdom in me, and my native dress was a reminder of the dignity of spirit to which I am rightfully bound, and I will try always to honor and respect it.

During the presentation, my son spoke to the anti-abortionists and asked them why they had come to protest. He learned that many of them had not read *Embraced*, and when he told them that I had been advised by my doctors to abort him and that I had chosen not to, they came in to apologize to me. I was grateful that I had quietly presented myself with respect while I wore my native dress and that I had been reminded to be humble at a time when the only gift that I could offer was love.

A Touch from Home

We have all had the experience of meeting someone whose spirit we recognize without quite knowing what to make of it. We know them. They know us. We recognize each other's souls when we look into each other's eyes and heart. When that happens, we may actually be recognizing that we knew each other before we ever came to this earth. Sometimes those feelings may come gradually, and there is no need for an immediate response to it; other times the reaction is an immediate desire to share our energy and celebrate the love between us now.

One woman, a soul friend who has gone to the spirit world since we met, described the sensation of looking into my eyes in words that still warm my heart: "A touch from home," she said. Our reconnecting of spirits took us both by surprise when we met for the first time here on earth. While sharing the message of *Embraced*, I met many bookstore managers and owners who were delighted to have me in their stores to autograph books. At one stop I was excited to meet yet another owner and arrived early to do so. Taking time to freshen myself in the ladies' room, I was absent when the owner arrived to greet me. I had learned before coming that she had not finished reading my book and that she normally didn't carry this *type* of book in her store. For some reason not known to us at the time, she had made an exception for *Embraced by the Light*. As I walked out of the rest room, she came toward me. Though we had never met, I "knew" her and I knew she "knew" me. Our eyes locked, and a recognition of each other's spirit filled our hearts with joy. Without saying a word, we ran into each other's arms and held each other like loved ones who had not seen each other for years.

"Betty, you made it, my little darlin'!" she wept, "and I'm so very proud of you." "Yes, I did, I did," was all that I could answer in response. My love for her and the delight of being in her arms overwhelmed me. Forgetting that I had been told that she had read only the first two chapters of my book, I was in total acceptance of what she went on to say: "Betty, I remember that you promised that you would do this, and this is an important part of your mission," she whispered to me.

Although I could not remember that promise as she had, my spirit remembered when she had promised me that she would be here for me as a mile marker to remind me that I was on the right path to accomplish my goals.

Remembering our lives together in the preexistence startled both of us, and although the veil was lifted back for us to remember, it lasted only a few short minutes. Our eternal bond was never forgotten, and we remained close friends on earth until she was called home.

I was shown in the spirit world that we bond not only in friendships but in families. Spirits who rejoin on earth in family groups were spirit friends united by a love for each other that had developed over eternities of togetherness. Often bonded in the work they can do together on earth, they come to earth knowing that they will meet here.

As soul friends, we promise each other in the spirit world that we will be close, but sometimes our journeys here on earth separate us until the proper time brings us together again. These times are opportunities we should always be open to seeing; they are chances to build on soul-satisfying relationships with spirits we'd been united with in a common purpose before this life.

When we do recognize our soulmates, we should look

for the deeper meaning for our bonding, not just to find it for ourselves—the ego's response to being on earth—but to find our common purpose that includes others in the world who we promised to help. The spirit is selfless, and the purpose that unites and bonds it to another is more powerful than ego.

Sometimes we recognize the soul friend before we recognize our purpose together. That purpose can become clear during the exchange of friendship, though where we are in our thoughts or our lives and our motives at the time can distort that reason or enhance it. When it's right, then we become energized. The magic happens. We work together, complete our mission, and it's perfect.

But sometimes the purpose does not present itself to us. To find it, each spirit must become attuned to the other, and both to God. It may be that one or the other spirit must develop further for the purpose to emerge. We can hold each other up in prayer until we both are at the same level to achieve our purpose. Often that development follows suffering, because we grow when we have lived through a painful experience. That experience is often preparatory to the work that is awaiting. We must trust our spirits to guide us. We must trust our hearts and pray to God that he will direct us, both of us, to the right path, if that is according to his divine will.

When we make connections, the results can be surprisingly powerful. Another example of that power happened when I made a connection with a soul friend who I think of fondly as another special angel. It happened after a tour in Chicago. I boarded the plane to fly home; I was exceptionally tired and ready for some quiet time and rest. Before I sat down, I glanced around and looked into the faces of the people with whom I would be sharing this space. I was curious about their destinations. I wondered if any of them had read *Embraced* and what they felt about life, death, and God. I found my seat by the window and breathed in feelings of contentment at finally being able to rest and reflect on the past three days of spiritual exchange.

Leaning back, I closed my eyes, but was abruptly disturbed by the sudden cries of a baby who was in the seat in front of me. Nervously, the father commented that the baby was missing her mother and that they were both anxious to get home to her. When the crying continued, I knew this was going to be a long ride home. Usually I brought plenty to read, but this time I had brought nothing. Giving up on the idea of being quietly entertained during my three and half hour flight back home, I glanced out the window hoping to catch a last glimpse of the beautiful waters of Lake Michigan and the towering buildings that I knew stood along its shore.

Suddenly, my attention was drawn to the more annoying sound of another child who was sitting directly behind me. She talked, but her words were garbled and her voice unusually loud and irritating. I raised myself up and looked over the seat as the sounds that had at first been abrasive began to seem melodic to me. In the seat behind me sat a young girl about the age of ten. Her bright blue eyes looked deep into mine. There was an immediate spiritual exchange between us. A chill ran through me, and my flesh rose in what I used to call goose bumps, but now refer to as spirit sparks, because they call your attention to an immediate recognition of spiritual awareness. The girl was obviously mentally retarded, I guessed from Down's syndrome. Turning back around in my seat, I sat with my eyes closed, listening to her as she communicated with my spirit. Only she and I knew that our spirits had transcended the mortal language barrier of this earth, and her communication with me was one of sweet pureness. "I'm doing my part," I understood her to say, "and you're a little bit behind on yours." I knew exactly what she was telling me.

After *Embraced* had been out for a year, I was told by the spirit to write the next book. I had begun to write it, but many other things kept me from finishing it, so I put it aside. A year later, I was awakened during the night and I was shown symbolically the universal clock that I had seen before during my journey into the spirit world; its regular ticking sounds now beat faster. I was told that the time had been shortened. I knew that whatever I needed to do had to be done more quickly. Although I still did not know fully what my mission entailed, I had prayed for guidance and "knew" that writing this book was next. But I was still busy bringing the message of *Embraced* to as many people as possible. My schedule had prevented me from taking the time I needed to write, and I still had many engagements on my calendar.

Feeling ashamed as I sat in the plane, I reached for my briefcase and pulled out my yellow tablet and a pen. I quickly began to write as I was inspired to. I knew that special people would be sent along at times to remind me of my continued journey and to keep me focused. I wrote feverishly, knowing that there was so much more for me to do—certainly more than I felt I could handle at the moment. But now thanks to my little angel's voice of encouragement, I had a new resolve and determination to move forward as quickly as possible. When the plane landed, I hurriedly rose from my seat to look into her eyes again. She smiled knowingly, raised her hand, and waved good-bye.

Often, when I am asked what I understand about reincarnation, I think about this little girl. Life on earth is like going away to college. Our spirits stay here until we graduate, then we leave the campus and go on to further our development elsewhere. Some graduating students can return if they have acquired enough knowledge to return as teachers. I thought of the spirits I had seen as they prepared to be born into the bodies of children whose lives would be short or challenged by handicap or illness. Their lights burned the brightest of all. I felt that this little girl with Down's syndrome was such a teacher, and I couldn't help but wonder how many other students she might have besides me.

I knew I would never see this special little angel again on earth, so as I walked away, I looked back at her for one last time. I was filled with the affirmation of God's tremendous love, not only for me, but for all his children. I whispered "Thank you" to this angel, thinking, "At some future date in heaven when we see each other again, we will reminisce about this meeting as soul friends."

The Courage to Live

When we leave ourselves open to God to learn more about unconditional love, he readily sends us the people we need to learn to love without judgment. Sometimes, our existing love is tested just so that we can see how unconditional it is. Put to the test without failure, our spirits expand with greater love, God's pure love, and it shines brighter within us. My love for a friend was tested when, one night after coming home from a speaking tour, I received a phone call from him.

Will and I had never met, even though we had been long-distance-telephone friends for over a year. Before the number of calls became too much to handle and I changed to an unlisted number, I received calls from many readers, and though few of those contacts led to lasting friendship, Will's call was one that did. I had sensed in him a great strength of character, and he expressed a tremendous love for God that drew me to him the first time we talked. His quick wit and sensitivity to me and my experience soon bonded him to me as one of my treasured friends. It became Will's habit to phone me after each speaking tour to inquire how things had gone. I fondly referred to him as a worrywart, because he always voiced his concern over the slightest infractions that he perceived might have occurred at my presentations. On this particular night I had plenty to tell him and I needed his advice.

"I think I met the audience that was the most challenging for me," I began. "Last night in New York, the audience was made up mostly of gay people, and their questions covered a lot of issues . . . especially about AIDS. Because of *Embraced*, I've had several opportunities to talk with people with AIDS, but I don't have answers to all their spiritual questions, and some of the people at the lecture were dissatisfied with the answers I gave them. I don't know, Will, it was difficult and exhausting for me. And after a while, those questioning me got rather demanding and angry. When I got back to my hotel room, I felt quite unsettled! I also realized I don't know very much about gay people."

God has wonderful ways of bringing light into each of our lives, and little did I know at this time that God had placed Will in my life for more reasons than friendship. I had grown to love Will like a brother, a caring one who teases and nags but is always there when "little sis" needs a hug over the phone.

As we continued to talk about how my lecture had gone, I noticed that Will was more reserved than usual. When I moved on to a different subject a few minutes later, he interrupted me. He sounded nervous, and I had not known him to act this way before.

"Going back to what we were talking about earlier, Betty . . . there's something I've never told you before, partly because I was afraid of your reaction." He paused, taking a long breath, then finished, "In case you haven't already figured it out, I'm gay."

Will and I knew each other pretty well by this time, and I had spoken to Will's roommate, Tim, a few times on the phone. Ordinarily, I would never have suspected that either Tim or Will was gay. Like a lot of people who haven't had much experience with gay people, when I thought about homosexuals, I tended to think in sterotypes. Although Will did not fit a stereotype, sometime earlier in our friendship I knew in my spirit that there was a possibility he was gay, even though Will had never said or done anything to make me suspect his sexual orientation. The possibility hadn't really mattered to me then, and the subject never came up. He was just Will to me, a friend who cared about me and brought me a lot of joy and happiness.

"Somehow, I already knew that you were gay, Will," I confessed in an accepting voice. I also "knew" that this moment of sharing was difficult for him.

"I kind of thought you did, but I wasn't sure," Will said. "I don't really try to hide the fact that I'm gay, but I don't go around broadcasting it either. I've been wanting to tell you for a long time, Betty. I didn't really think you would disapprove and tell me I was going to hell, but since we hadn't talked about it, I wasn't completely sure."

My heart wanted to reach out to Will as I sensed his discomfort; I wanted him to know my feelings for him hadn't changed. We had shared a lot of personal details with each other about our lives, and the trust of friendship had been firmly established in both of us. I knew he now felt that he might have damaged that trust by keeping his homosexuality secret from me. "You worry too much, you old worrywart! My spirit told me a long time ago that you were 'different,'" I joked, wanting to lighten things a little, while wishing this subject had not come up. "We are still friends," I reassured him, suddenly wanting some reassurance myself. "Aren't we?"

"Sure," he said. I could hear the relief in his voice. "It's just that it took me years to reconcile being gay and a Christian, and I would have been crushed if you had said it was a sin to be gay, because I know in my heart it isn't."

"Will, you are God's creation, just like me and every-one else," I offered my assurance.

"Exactly," he replied. "But most Christians don't feel that way." Then he added in a pensive voice, "I've thought and prayed about this a lot, and I know in my heart God made me this way. As a matter of fact if I weren't gay, I'd probably be one of those fundamentalist ministers who is convinced he has all the answers and I would never have been open to the message of God's unconditional love in *Embraced*. It took me a long time to make peace with my sexual orientation, and it wasn't easy. I got so overwhelmed at one point that I actually tried to kill myself."

"Oh, Will!" I said, shocked to hear that my loving friend had once attempted suicide. All I could think of was what a loss it would have been for all of us who have been touched by his love and what a terrible spiritual tragedy it would have been for him. "I would never have thought you could try to kill yourself, Will."

"I'm not proud of it," he replied in a sober voice. "But I did."

As his voice trailed off, I began to pray for understanding, and for the next half hour, Will went on to tell me how he struggled to reconcile his sexuality and his faith. Growing up in a fundamentalist church, he taught Sunday school, was active in the youth group, and even preached on several occasions; he decided in high school that God was calling him to become a minister. "Everyone knew I was going to become a preacher, and they began treating me like one," he said. "And then, when I was eighteen, my life started unraveling."

When he realized that an attraction to one of his male classmates wasn't going away, he began to wonder if he was gay—and was filled instantly with shame. "Because of my religious upbringing, I hadn't even thought about sex for most of my teen years," he said. "Being homosexual was just about the worst thing that could happen to me. Over and over again, I got down on my knees, crying and praying for hours for God to help me. But nothing worked."

I could identify immediately with the despair of unanswered prayers and the tests they can put on our faith. "I was sure I had been called to be a minister, and yet I knew that could never happen if I remained a homosexual," he continued. "I felt like a hypocrite when I went to church. I got severely depressed and wound up losing my scholarship and dropping out of college. Eventually, I gave up my plans to enter the ministry." After four years of struggle, he told me, he finally accepted that "no amount of wishing or praying or willpower was going to change" his homosexual feelings.

"I still didn't want to live my life as a homosexual," he said. "And I was afraid of what would happen to me in the next life if I did. Even though I had been 'born again,' every church I had been to said homosexuals couldn't go to heaven." Isolated from his family and his church, his depression deepened into self-hatred. "I felt helpless, empty and hollowed out, like my soul was being smothered by darkness. There was a voice in the darkness that started telling me the only way out was suicide. By this time I was in such despair that I didn't even think about the afterlife anymore. I just wanted to turn myself off and get away from the pain."

By this time, Will continued, his struggle had come to the notice of his doctor, who prescribed Valium. "I abused the prescription, taking more than he had prescribed," remembered Will. "Then one day when I just couldn't stand it anymore, I took the rest of the bottle and lay down on my bed, expecting never to wake up."

It was hard to take in everything that Will was telling me; I felt his pain so deeply. For while I had never contemplated suicide, in my darkest days I had known how it felt to have lost one's will to live. I thought of "David Stone," who had called in such desperation on the verge of his own suicide. As I considered Will's suicide attempt, I shuddered to imagine that such a fine man of God had almost wasted his capacity to share as much love as I knew him to have.

My love for Will welled up in me, and I rejoiced in the ripple effect that his living through his troubles had set in motion, thanks to his sharing his light as generously as he always did. At the same time, it was hard for me to resist being angry, angry that the name of God had been used by others to bring a child of God to such a dark place in his life. Jesus's message is that we are all to love one another; we are not to presume to choose which of God's children are unworthy of his love. Only God knows the hearts of man. Any church that places itself in the seat of God, as judge, is committing what was shown to me as the greater sin by placing fear and guilt between us and God. The fact that a church would attempt to do this in his name made clear once again how urgent it is for all of us to spread God's message of love.

Will survived, and although his actions strained to the breaking point his already difficult relations with his family, he slowly began to mend—and learn. "I still hadn't resolved my spiritual dilemma, but the worst part of the crisis passed," he said. "I had also learned one important lesson: Trying to kill myself was the most stupid and selfish thing I had ever done, and I knew I would never do it again!" He told me that he knows that he will have to experience the pain and anxiety he caused his family and friends at his life review, and that, through years of effort, he and his family have been able to find forgiveness for the pain they inflicted on each other leading up to and following his suicide attempt.

I knew that, along the way, Will had somehow also learned to forgive himself—for his selfish act and for his not turning out the way he had thought he needed to be to live the life he had wanted. I could see that he had brought into his life the power of some of the spiritual laws that I had been taught—that forgiveness of ourselves is where all forgiveness starts, because we can't love others if we don't first love ourselves, and that if we are to overcome the hardships that we will inevitably face, we must accept all of our experiences as good, however bad they seem, for they help us in the spiritual growth we are here on earth to accomplish. Thinking of how different the Will I knew was from the young man he was describing, I understood what he had done, but I wondered how he had done it. "You must have made peace with yourself and with God since then," I said, hoping he would explain how he did so and how God had led the way.

"Yes, I did, eventually," Will replied. "My brush with death opened my eyes and prepared my heart to receive some answers that had been there all along. After I asked God to forgive me, he used three very special friends to lead me to him." First was a Baptist woman whose family took him in after his own rejected him. "Her unconditional love showed me that at least one devout Christian could accept me for who I was. Another friend, a gay man, took the next healing step further by demonstrating that homosexuality and spirituality weren't necessarily opposed to each other, something I desperately needed to know." Finally, his Lutheran minister overcame his discomfort when Will revealed the reason for his suicide attempt and accepted him as a friend and coworker in the church. "Knowing that a pastor could value a gay man as a bona fide Christian told me that maybe what I had been taught in the other churches was wrong," Will said.

I could feel the anguish in Will's voice and the bottled-up pain that finally found its way outside of him. Wanting to let him continue without my interruptions, I sat silently listening.

"Still, it was a gradual process that required a lot of prayer and soul-searching. Finally, it was my own inner voice that told me I didn't have to be straight to be a Christian, and I didn't have to abandon my faith to be gay. I realized I had never felt any judgment from God, only from some Christians. And when I examined my heart, I could feel God's love and I could feel my own love for him. Like most gay people, I knew I had never *chosen* to be gay, which meant to me that God had made me that way. I still didn't know his reasons, but I realized I had to make peace with being gay before I could get on with my life.

"In the years since my attempted suicide, I've managed to build a good life for myself, with God's help. I have the career I wanted and terrific friends. And I found a wonderful partner who gives me love and support and opens my eyes to truths I had never stopped to examine before. If God hadn't given me a second chance, I would have missed all that. But he did, and I have felt his unwavering love for me every step of the way. I need no other proof to convince me that I am as he made me, and he loves me because of it.

"I have always believed God has a reason for everything. Now I can look back at my life and see some of the reasons he made me this way. Everything I am, especially my spirituality, is a direct result of my struggle to accept my sexual orientation. It forced me to question religious assumptions and open my heart to spiritual truth instead. And most important of all, it made me understand the absolute importance of unconditional love."

"There it is again," I thought. "Unconditional love, the test in all our lives that brings us to greater understanding of ourselves." As I had listened to Will, I was reminded of the judgments that I, myself, had made about homosexuals. Will taught me what a toxic impact those judgments can have on them and how the fear of rejection can undermine their self-esteem. I had been shown that by judging others, we display the shortcomings in ourselves. Only God is the judge, and we are all precious and watched over by the loving eyes of God.

Will told me that more faiths are beginning to open their hearts more acceptingly, making it possible for gay people to nurture their faith by joining a body of believers. The ripple effect of their determination to find God in spite of the fact that they are often told that he is not there for them is quite powerful. The ripple effect can push others to find their own way, whatever the difficulties.

As for me, my love for my friend did not change; in fact, we grew closer. Will's humility, courageous struggle, and greater love for our Father in heaven have bonded our friendship forever.

Prayers and Forgiveness

I was shown in the spirit world that each of us has been given the ability to reach God with our prayers. I saw the angels as they flew from person to person, rushing to answer the prayers as they shot up from the earth like beacons of light. They took such joy in their work and rejoiced, too, that they had been asked. Whatever form it takes, each prayer is an invitation for God to bring his power into another life. God wants to help us, but he waits for us to seek his help.

A group of priests and nuns had asked me one day if I would spend some time visiting some very ill people in their hospital. My day was free, so there was no question I would accept. Service is the best way to pass on the love we share and open ourselves to the love we have to receive . . . it is the oil that lights our lamps. In my darkest days years ago, service had helped me begin to heal, and as a counselor and volunteer worker in later years, it had brought me closer to God. If I had the opportunity to help others heal their souls in time of struggle, I could hardly say no.

I was waiting in front of my hotel that morning when a long, black limousine pulled up to the curb. I couldn't help but notice it, and as the rear door opened, I wondered what kind of person was going to step out. I wasn't prepared for what I saw: a nun, in full habit, and she was looking for me.

I quickly learned that Sister Rose was a delightful woman. She had a tremendous sense of humor and a heart full of love. We crawled into the cavernous, dark passenger compartment of the limo, and she explained that the vehicle had been donated for the day by a local mortuary. As the car pulled away from the curb, I realized I didn't really know much about where we were going; all I knew was that I was being whisked across town in the rear of an enormous limo, on the way to a hospital, with a lovely, funny nun. As always, I knew that God had put me in the right place.

When we got to the hospital, a priest met us at the door of the unit we were visiting. He told me that many of the patients we would see were dying from AIDS. I knew then that the people I would see would be in great need of relief from their pain and of assurance of God's love, and I mentally prepared myself.

I had treated and counseled people with AIDS before I began speaking in public about my near-death experience. I had come to know their concerns from both my clinic and my volunteer work, and I had helped many young men confront mortality at an early age. When *Embraced* was published, I discovered many of them were drawn to its message of hope and love. Thinking now of the struggle with the church that my friend Will had told me about, I was glad that the message could reach people who might feel that they could not find spirituality within the structure of traditional religion.

I assumed that the patients I was about to see had read *Embraced* and wanted to spend some time with me. I thought they might want reassurance that its message could be shared by them and that the glorious welcome I received awaits them when they return to their spiritual home. I knew I could tell them what I've told other people with AIDS: Their suffering is no different from any earthly suffering. It is not God's punishment to them, as some of them have learned to fear, and we can all develop spiritually by sharing our love freely with those who are suffering. Their faith, their love of God, and their love for themselves can be as powerful as medicine in their healing process.

When the priest brought me into the first room, I prayed for the ability to bring some comfort and love. He introduced me to the gentleman in the bed and asked him if he wanted to spend some time alone with me. When the patient said that he did, the priest stepped out of the room and we visited for a few moments, but the patient had little to say. When the priest returned moments later, we left. The brief visit left me feeling uncomfortable and unsure of what my purpose for being there was.

In the next room, the priest stepped out again. I looked through the door's little window and saw him leaning with his back against the door. Praying for some direction from God, I was inspired to ask this patient if there was anything I could do for him. When he shook his head no, I asked if he'd like me to pray with him. This got a positive response, the first I had seen, so I began to pray, ending my prayer with a simple *amen*—only to see a look of disappointment on the patient's face.

When I was left alone again with the third patient, I remembered the previous patient's reaction to the prayer. I realized that, this being a Catholic hospital, these patients must be Catholic. Having been a Catholic decades ago, I remembered that a Catholic's prayer ends with the sign of the cross; this time when I finished my prayer, I made the sign of the cross, and the patient completed it with me. For the first time that day, I felt that I had been able to help these souls find what they were looking for.

It had been years since I had even attempted to make

the sign of the cross. Its simple gestures immediately took me back to my childhood in Catholic school, when I struggled to remember the order in which I was supposed to make the four gestures of crossing myself. In my mind, I was there on my knees, fumbling in front of a nun from the school who was holding a long stick over me. If I did it out of order, she would tap me on the head with the rubber ball at the point of the stick. For some reason, it was hard for me to learn, and I got tapped a lot—sometimes more than a tap.

By the time I visited the last of the patients, watching them as they performed the sign with me, I had gotten it right once again.

We discovered that we had finished a little ahead of schedule. Sister Rose told me that there was another hospital across town we could visit, but we would have to bypass a lunch they had planned for us at a nice local restaurant. I couldn't refuse to go to the hospital, so we climbed back into the limo to ride through midday traffic. This time we shared a bucket of chicken, riding through town with a paper tablecloth stretched between us—mine tucked into my dress, hers into her habit—to keep our visiting outfits (and the borrowed limo) clean.

She told me how much she had appreciated *Embraced*, even with its depiction of my struggle with the Catholic church as a child, when I was continuing to search on earth for the loving God I had met in heaven as a very young girl. She apologized to me for all of the hurt that I might have received from what she felt was the misconduct of people in authority within the Catholic church. "But that's how it was back then," she added. "They were doing what they thought was right."

At the second hospital, where I could now perform the sign of the cross quite smoothly, I noticed that the patients were very comfortable with my presence. I reflected, too, on the love that flowed so freely between the patients and the priest at the first hospital. It occurred to me that it doesn't matter whether we wear a cross around our necks or make the sign of the cross or light candles. Whatever manner in which we choose to communicate with God is not important; these are the mechanical touchstones that we use in our faith, and if we're doing what we think is right, there is a value in that. But what is more important than anything else, ever, is simply that we make that communication with God from the very depths of our heart and, when we share it with another person, that we do so with the purity of spirit of unconditional love.

It simply isn't possible to say or learn too much about prayer. I was thinking about that soon afterward, at an evening presentation, when the topic of suicide came up in a question from the audience, as it frequently does. As always, I was reminded of the man I knew as "David Stone." I had not heard from him since our phone call, and though I often prayed for him and continued to put his "name" on the prayer list, I wondered what had happened to him. The thought that there was nothing I could do to help him now, that he had taken his life after he had hung up, continued to torment me; I thought of the ripple effect that his suicide would set into motion—its damage spreading to his family, his children, and on and on—and I prayed for the many people in its path.

I spoke of "David" in many presentations when the issue of suicide was raised. I told many people of his ravaged soul, of the pain that can bring a person to the point of taking his own life, and of my hope that "David" would listen to God. I spoke of the temendous power of prayer that was required for such a hardened heart and of our need to support our loved ones in prayer. I shared openly about our encounter, and as time went on I realized that the audience could sense my grief and my disappointment in the limits of my skills to help this man. It was difficult for all of us, but I could tell that people benefited from his story, so I continued to share it.

I had spoken of him again the evening that my traveling companion, Georgia, told me minutes after the presentation that someone wanted to talk to me before I began signing books. "I know you don't usually have time for this, but I think you're going to be interested in this man," she said. "He says he's 'David Stone.'"

At first I was stunned. And then I didn't believe it. I knew that anyone who wanted to attract my attention could say he was "David Stone." But feeling I should make sure, I walked with Georgia over to where the man was standing. His face was red, and his eyes full of tears. I could see him trembling as I walked toward him, and he held his arms open for an embrace long before I got to him. One look at his face told me that he was indeed my "David Stone."

I was relieved to see him. But I had lived through so much pain not knowing whether he had taken his life, pain that he could have relieved by making contact and letting me know that he was okay, that somehow I felt betrayed by him. He had called me because he had a need, and I was there for him. And then once that need was filled, he was gone. So while I gave him an embrace, wondering what I was going to say to him, I was feeling more than just love.

"I'm David, Betty, and you saved my life," he said as I pulled away from him. And I told him how I felt.

"David, I'm so angry at you right now," I said. "Why didn't you call me? I have lived in agony."

"You know, I knew you cared, because I got your book and I read it," he said. "And I know you are a caring woman. But it wasn't until I heard you tonight, when you shared the story of 'David Stone,' me, my story, that I realized just how much you cared. I'm sorry. But you can see that I'm fine."

My anger cooled, and I listened to his story.

"After hanging up from you—and I had not read your

book—I thought I at least owed it to myself to read *Embraced* before I took my life," he said. "Many of the things that you said to me caught my interest. And I wanted to know what else you had to say. So I went out and bought the book, brought it home. And I read it and realized, for the first time in my life, that I have a purpose that is far greater than I knew. And although I couldn't see it at that time, I had to give myself back to God.

"I turned myself around," he continued. "I was still in grief; I was still dark; I was still in despair. It took me a long time. I prayed for God to help, every day."

My heart went out to him. I thought of my own long struggle out of darkness and knew how hard it must have been to keep praying for God's help when there was no sign it was working, and how hard it was to learn that we must let go of our prayers and let God answer them. I knew he had taken the difficult steps he needed to move on. By admitting his mistakes to himself, he had repented; by letting go, he had forgiven himself and become able to accept that God had forgiven him long ago.

"Now my life isn't—" he hesitated, then continued, "as I had first prayed that it would be. I didn't receive my wife back. I visit my children. I have my mother and my father. I'm back in church now." He hesitated again, his speech slowing. "My whole life is different. But somehow I'm stronger in God than I have ever been in my life. And if that was God's purpose, to let me fall to the bottom of the pit in order to come out more secure, stronger in every way, then for that I'm grateful—and to you, all my life."

And then I could embrace him with all my heart. He continued talking. I was just pleased to look at his face and know that he really was fine. But people had begun to gather around us, also seeking attention. I reached out to him one more time. I wanted to tell him that I didn't know his real name. But the crowd was beginning to divide us, and he disappeared into it.

I never did learn his name. I'll continue to think of him as "David Stone." And I'll never forget that last exchange—where a soul looks into another soul, and they touch each other's lives. I knew that at some point I had promised to be there for him, and when he needed me, that day on the phone, my voice was something he could cling to. Although he had only heard my voice, he had felt my spirit, just as I had felt his. Whatever purpose we had for each other's lives, we fulfilled. When we needed each other, we were there.

Letting Go

I hear from thousands of men, women, and children who are eager to tell me of their own near-death experiences. It is a wonderful source of joy for me to connect, however briefly, with other experiencers who are willing to share what they have learned about God. The love that they experienced radiates from them and nourishes me each time I hear a new story. I am also strengthened by the knowledge that sharing my experience has helped others to share theirs, setting into motion the ripple effect of the love that is spread by countless people as they pass on the message of God's love.

Even more people come to me in pain, grieving over

the loss of a loved one. I know the pain of loss; I have buried an infant daughter and lost other family members, including my mother. I was present at the death my dad. I still miss them all. They are on a long journey without me now, and knowing that they are all together, I wish at times that I were with them. But I do not grieve for them. Life on this earth as mortal beings was never meant to continue forever. We are here for only a season, and then we go home. . . .

When I can, I try to help by sharing that message with people who come to me tormented by grief. The loss of someone you love can be painful, and recovery from it is a difficult challenge. The most intense pain that I have seen comes from people who have lost loved ones to long, debilitating illnesses. Frequently after resuscitation, the dying are kept alive artificially for extended periods of time. Medical care today can do a lot to maintain life in a body that is unable to live on its own. There are more people than ever facing the difficult decision we faced with my dad—the decision to let go.

Many people must make this decision, as we did with Dad, to let their loved one's body die. *Not* removing loved ones from the machines or *not* halting the procedures that maintain the *signs* of physical life in their body is often a selfish act.

Letting go is different from euthanasia. In euthanasia drugs are administered for the purpose of ending a life that is still sustaining itself; that is much like suicide and is a violation of the universal laws I was shown. Ending a life brings about a premature end to the spirit's time on earth. That soul is here to learn the lessons that we all came to this world to learn or to teach. Life should not be shortened but should be allowed to exist until its appointed time. I saw that spirits will stay near their bodies until they are released from them, anxious to go on. If life is sustained *only* by man-made inventions, then releasing it from that invention and letting that person go naturally, with drugs to aid pain, can be the ultimate act of love.

For some survivors, peace does not come easily. I have met loving people who are overwhelmed with doubt about whether they made the right choice. Guilt generally follows that decision to let someone you love die. That pain of guilt is unnecessary and unfounded. When our decision to let a loved one go is made with prayer and purity of heart, then we are obeying the most fundamental law of all, to love one another as we would love ourselves, and we will eventually receive in kind.

Because of their love for us, those we love can often find a way to express their love and gratitude to us long after their souls have left this earth. Many who make their transition will try to make contact right away, and we can receive that communication when we are ready to accept it.

Faith and forgiveness are the gifts we have to help us get through the pain of any loss, especially the loss of a life that ends after man prolongs it. But for some the test of faith is almost too difficult. Many survivors whose grief is so powerful tell me that they fear they have lost their will to live. One of those survivors came into my life just recently. I was drawn to Sherrie's letter, and when I called her, she said that the call came during her darkest moments of despair. I'm glad that I reached out to her and grateful for her willingness to share her experience with others. Knowing that it is okay to let go, perhaps more people will begin to heal.

Sherrie wrote to me a few months after burying her husband, at a time, she said, when she was searching for answers "that neither doctors, priests, family, nor friends could provide." Sherrie was living with the life-and-death decisions she had made concerning her husband, who, after eleven months in a coma, made his transition to the other side following her decision not to continue the treatment that had sustained him. "I knew that the person lying there connected to all of mankind's inventions was not the person I had loved for so long," she wrote. "Even though I knew deep down that I had done everything possible for him, I still wondered if I had done enough."

When I called her, I could feel the depth of her despair—the fear that she had made the wrong decision and the loneliness in which she suffered that fear. Our spirits connected that day I called, and I knew why I had been led to her, and she to me. Even over the telephone,

I could sense our exchange of energy, as we shared the magic of unconditional love. I encouraged her to tell me her story. She was grateful for the opportunity to do so, and my heart went out to her.

Sherrie had met her first love, Len, when they were both teenagers, over twenty years ago. They married, had two children, remained deeply in love, and "life went on normally" until Len suffered his first heart attack, about six years ago, and their "little world came crashing down." After a hospital stay, he had four years of good health, until a test in early 1994 revealed "a few things that the doctor said he'd keep an eye on."

A few weeks after that test, Sherrie began to sense that their time together might be drawing to an end. Alone in the house one afternoon, she woke up from a nap crying over a dream that her husband had died. "Just then I heard a voice, as if someone were whispering in my ear, 'It's going to happen this year,'" she recalled. "I was quite shaken, as he had been doing so well. I tried to dismiss it as nothing but a bad dream, but it was not to be so easy."

Len suffered his second heart attack the following month, which necessitated a seven-way bypass operation. The surgery was successful, and Len came off the respirator the next morning, but he then came down with pneumonia and was put into an induced coma and back on the respirator for another week. "Miraculously, he came out of that fine," said Sherrie. It took several months to recover to the point that he could return to work, but within a month of his doing so, he suffered a third attack that destroyed half of his heart.

"He would not recuperate this time," said Sherrie. "He became more tired and more weak each day." The months rolled by as Len's health declined. One day in early October, as he was helping his sister prepare for a Halloween party, he drew a sketch of a witch with her tongue sticking out on his desk calendar, filling the space for a day that at the time was still in the future; the rest of the calendar was blank. Sherrie didn't discover this sketch until a few days after that date had passed. By then she knew that it was the date on which Len suffered his final heart attack at home—the day on which, according to Sherrie, "he died for the first time."

After spending the morning and afternoon with Len, she had left to pick up their son from football practice. Within twenty minutes, she returned to discover Len in the agony of his attack. "I called 911 and they came within five minutes. I did not know it at the time, but my husband had died before they arrived. They put him in the ambulance, and we proceeded to the hospital while they administered CPR and brought him back to life. At one point we had to pull over, and I tried to see what was happening in the back. The driver would not let me see, and all of a sudden I felt a surge of warm energy flush through my whole body, head to toe. When it was over, I felt very weak and numb."

After they arrived at the emergency room, several hours of intense effort passed before Sherrie was permitted to return to her husband's side. "When they allowed me to go back and see him, I knew in my heart that he was gone," she told me. "That poor, defenseless person with all the tubes running in and out of him was not my husband anymore. I knew, but I still prayed for a miracle."

Len remained in a coma for the next eleven months, during which he continued to deteriorate and was shuttled from hospital to nursing home to emergency room and back as the crises mounted. "I can't count the many hours I spent in the emergency room and by his bedside," said Sherrie.

Finally, he was struck by a powerful pneumonia that resisted antibiotics, and Sherrie was faced with her decision—whether to put Len through the trauma of a surgical procedure to facilitate the IV administration of antibiotics or to let him die peacefully with comfort care. "This was the hardest decision of my life," remembered Sherrie. After consulting with doctors and priests, she chose the latter.

"I sat with Len day and night for eight days watching him die. I had asked a very kind nurse if I could get into bed with Len just to hold him one last time. She closed the door and gave us privacy. I very carefully slid into bed next to Len and put my arm around him. I told him that it was time to go to heaven, and he opened his eyes and stared upward toward the ceiling. When he would open his eyes like this, I often wondered if he was seeing something that I could not. He kept blinking and staring, and I asked him if he was seeing his great-grandmother, whom he had been close to and who had passed away many years ago. I told him to go with her, that it was okay and everything would be all right. I kissed him good-bye and told him that I loved him and that I always would. He then closed his eyes and went to sleep.

"I went back the next morning and was told that I could no longer suction him, as I was only prolonging the eventual outcome. I told the nurse that I could not stay then. I was at a point where I was very near breaking down completely. I told the hospital to call me when it was over. Len died peacefully the next morning. No struggle, just one last breath. The nurses told me that they thought he was waiting to make sure I would not be there when it happened."

Then began Sherrie's final struggle—to find peace with herself with her decision. "My mind and heart could not accept it," she said. "I felt as if my life had ended, too. I didn't know how to start over without him. And the guilt was never-ending."

When Sherrie and I spoke, I assured her that she was not alone, that thousands of people go through much the same situation, and that she still had a purpose in this life. We spoke of letting go of our loved ones, and I told her that Len may have already said his good-byes to her when she felt that warm feeling in the back of the ambulance as the emergency workers struggled to bring him back. I have heard from other people who have experienced similar feelings, as if the soul is reaching out to a person that they love to let that person know that they are leaving.

I told her that Len's spirit was perhaps reaching out to her before then, too, when he made a drawing on the desk calendar for the day on which his spirit first tried to leave his body. The spirit can sometimes know that the time for its rebirth in death is approaching—and can sometimes know in advance, as Len did, the very day it will happen. My own father knew his time was near and let me know as I gave him his final haircut. I took comfort in Dad's knowing and encouraged Sherrie to take comfort in Len's, to see it as his attempt to let her know that his spirit saw his physical death coming and understood it for what it was, the passage to another stage of spiritual growth.

I hear of many spirits reaching out in this way to loved ones, sometimes even letting them know not just when they will die but how. After a speaking engagement, I met a grieving mother named Shirley, whose teenage daughter, Jenny, had been killed a month earlier. Jenny had told her mother shortly before the tragedy that she had always feared she would be murdered. At the time, Shirley was shocked by her daughter's statement and tried to comfort her; only in retrospect did she realize that Jenny's spirit may, in fact, have been trying to comfort Shirley. Just a few weeks before her death, Shirley told me, Jenny had put her affairs in order, going through her belongings and donating many to charity; she saw many members of her large extended family in the days before she was killed by her ex-boyfriend, in a crime to which he confessed. Shirley has no doubt that Jenny's spirit knew that her time on earth was coming to its end, and she has been able to turn her grief into action, making presentations on the topics of abusive relationships and teen date violence in schools throughout her area. She calls the presentation "Jenny's message."

Sherrie later shared a story with me that suggested that Len had one more message for her. "I collect these little cherubs called Dreamsicles," she told me. "After I buried my husband, this one little Dreamsicle would move on its own. It never happened while we were watching, but we would notice it would be turned as if someone had moved its position while we were looking the other way. I would turn it back, and the next day it would be turned around again. This went on for months. I actually kind of liked thinking it was Len, still around, keeping close to me and the kids. However, I remembered what we had talked about regarding needing to 'let go' of our loved ones so that they could proceed on their journey to heaven. So I said, 'Okay, Len, you can go now.

I don't want you to stay here with me any longer. It's time to move on.' The Dreamsicle has not moved since."

I was glad that Sherrie had been open to the possibility that Len was trying to reach her. Many spirits try to contact loved ones from time to time—when we need them. They appear to us in ways we can accept. We're most accessible to them when we are dreaming or meditating, but their visits can take many forms. I've been visited on several occasions. My mother came to me shortly before Dad's death. Joe's great-grandparents, whose names I didn't even know, appeared one night when I was researching my genealogy. Joe was frustrated that his lineage was hard to trace, because so many records had been destroyed over the years. One night while Joe was sleeping, they appeared and told me their name. They spelled their last name for me. We were later able to confirm it through information we otherwise never would have sought.

My visits with spirits have had a lasting effect on me; they can bring our lives a great deal of joy. I'll treasure the memory of the day in church when I heard the voice of my daughter, Cynthia, whom I lost to SIDS (sudden infant death syndrome) when she was three months old. Still, I recognized her voice in the chapel, over twenty years later, when she said to me, "Mother, I love you." I was going through a difficult time, not long after my return to earth. I'll always thank God for the gift of hearing her distinctive voice, given to me at a special time when I needed it.

I always tell people who want to know if they can contact their deceased loved ones that they can, and the way that I do it is to pray and ask God if it is necessary and if it is his will. It may not be his will for us to hear from a loved one, especially if doing so might encourage us to become so focused on our grief that we can't move on. The veil of forgetfulness that God sent us here with is an important part of our eternal growth on earth. I've seen its power in my own life, where the spirits of loved ones are involved. When I returned from my experience, I knew that I had been greeted by the spirits of loved ones, but I had no memory of my mother and daughter Cynthia being there. I just accepted that it was God's will that I not see them, but I did sometimes wonder what happened to them. Finally, I prayed, and he explained that they had been present, but I was not allowed to remember, that I wouldn't have overcome the depression that followed my return from the spirit world had I been able to recall that visit with them and the joy that I felt in their presence. Now that I can recall our reunion, the joy we shared is a source of strength for me today.

Sherrie told me that she can still find strength in her husband's presence, too. "Whenever I need his help, all I need to do is close my eyes and say, 'Help me do this, Len,'" she said, adding that she is then able to accomplish whatever she is trying to do. Sherrie's spirit has experienced tremendous healing since she opened her heart to the love that her beloved husband still has to offer, a love that guided her out of the darkness of fear and doubt in which she had been trapped. "I cherish my twenty-two years of marriage," she told me, "and the memories of a man who loved me enough to somehow send me help from above."

A Walking Miracle

Sometimes God will give us a miracle just to
remind us that he can. He wants us all to know that we
are his children and that his love is there for us. It is ours
to accept, our decision to make. He has given us free will
to make the choice for ourselves. When I was shown the
heavens scrolling back to reveal the earth and its billions
of people finding love, experimenting, and making mistakes, I knew that it is up to us to make the biggest
decision to choose for ourselves, each of us, if we want to
open our hearts to him and his love.

I saw, also, that those of us whose hearts have been
awakened to God have a responsibility to share his love
with others, as they make their own decisions. That is the

nature of service and of love; all of our lights shine brighter when we pass them along.

I need no further proof of God's awesome power and mighty love than what I saw and felt during my experience. I need no encouragement to tell people of the light I saw more brilliant than the sun or the dazzling life and clarity of the waterfall in his vibrant garden or his tangible, loving presence that fills the vastness of space, in which he has placed his many, far-flung worlds. But we are not all shown such wonders in this life; not all of us have come to believe that his help is there for the asking. For those of us who still doubt his existence and awesome power, God offers all of the evidence of his love and his glory that we need—at times, in the form of miracles.

I met one of those miracles in a community college parking lot on a hot Texas evening, when a joyous man picked me up off the ground, spun me around, and told me he loved me, over and over again, in an accent so thick I could barely understand him. I could feel his love immediately. I could tell I was in the presence of a man who had accepted the love God has to offer and is eager to spread the word to others, and I wanted to find out more.

The man's name is George, and he comes from Russia, where the story that he told me that night took place. Of the many near-death experiences I have heard, his is among the most miraculous and the most inspiring. He is a walking miracle, and his experience and his dedication to sharing it with as many others as possible touched my heart deeply. He is truly a man of God, and I was grateful to have the chance to learn more from him.

George had lived under the suppressive communist regime of the Soviet Union, from which he was about to escape when he was killed in a hit-and-run accident. Orphaned, adopted, and orphaned again, George had been an exceptionally bright student, he explained, graduating from the University of Moscow with a medical degree at the age of nineteen. But he had also been a dissident since his early teens, so the Soviet government long refused his requests to travel to America. After he started a family, the authorities, apparently convinced he would return, finally granted his request. He was waiting for the cab that would take him to the airport when he saw a car bearing down on him and soon found himself in a "darkness blacker than anything a human eye can imagine."

George's training did not prepare him for what he experienced next, when he realized he was no longer in his body and could find no scientific explanation for this. "I asked myself, How can I *be* when I don't have a body?'" he told me. "How can I see when I don't have eyes, and how can I think when I don't have a brain?"

Soon, he continued, he saw a light, but the fact that it appeared to be "outside of the darkness" confused him.

"What was happening to me was impossible," he told me. "My beliefs were based on the laws of physics and concrete, scientific facts, and everything I was experiencing was contrary to everything I knew."

At first, as George kept looking for a rational explanation for what he was seeing and feeling, the light was no more comforting than the darkness had been. Finally, he became part of the light and was filled with wave after wave of "the purest form of love, above what our human minds can comprehend," he explained. "And I began to feel that what was happening to me was right. I belonged here, and my fear was leaving. I felt energized but, at the same time, so peaceful, and satisfied beyond my wildest imagination."

He then understood that the light was knowledge, and sensing that great knowledge was being made available to him, he asked to be shown his body. It was still under the car he had seen coming toward him.

He watched as his body was taken by ambulance to the hospital, where surgeons tried unsuccessfully to resuscitate him. He watched his wife learn that he had been killed and saw that everything would be all right with his family, that they did not need him to continue their existence. "I did not feel sad anymore not to be in my body," he said. "I even looked at it and wondered how I could have lived there."

George traveled in spirit to visit other loved ones on

earth, including his dearest friend, whose wife was giving birth to their first child. It was there that George was able not only to understand someone's thoughts but also to make himself understood. The infant girl was crying uncontrollably, despite the doctor's efforts to comfort her, until George communicated to her to stop crying, and to everyone's surprise, she suddenly did. No one else could see George, nor did they know he was there. "I asked her if she understood me, and she communicated yes," George said. "I told her that they could not understand her, and she let me know her hip had twisted during her birth and was broken. I told her I wished they would understand, but until they did, to cry if it helped."

Much of what George told me that happened next reminded me of my own experience, when God's plan of creation came to me, and I rejoiced with the angels at its perfection. Similar to my own remembering of knowledge that had been hidden at birth by the "veil" of forgetfulness, George was allowed to receive pure knowledge, in which every question within his being was answered not just with words or pictures but with his participation in every event. He experienced a life review, in which he saw his own birth and learned the circumstances of his birth parents' death. He was also shown a detailed history of religion and of creation itself. "If I was part of an event, I was in the event," he told me. "If not, I was there observing with all senses each event.

I was able to receive and understand all thoughts involved in everything I was a part of."

As caught up in his story as I was—my heart fills with joy when others tell me of their encounters with the love and light that I so vividly remember—by now some of what George had said caused me to wonder just how much time had passed during his experience. His answer was astonishing, even to me.

"When I was out of body, I realized that time is not real, and I could not understand the reason for measuring it," he said. "I understood that it was Friday when I was hit by the car and taken to the morgue and an autopsy was scheduled for Monday, to comply with Soviet policies regarding unnatural death. It did not look good that a bright young scientist with an American visa in his pocket was killed by a hit-and-run driver."

It was during the very first stages of the autopsy that George suddenly returned to his body. "I felt a force grab the back of my neck and push me instantly down," he said. "I was just hurled down instantaneously."

George is certainly not the first person I've met who returned to his body after entering the morgue, although a four-day experience ending on the autopsy table is unusual. But it's not as scary as it might sound. I have heard from enough near-death experiencers to know that it is not important to the person who comes back how they come back to the body. It's not frightening to them. Like a person who goes into shock and doesn't feel certain things that they otherwise would feel, we are sweetly anesthetized by God's love, so that we don't experience the trauma.

Such was the case with George, who felt no fear as he realized what was happening, just a fierce determination to let them know he wasn't dead. When he succeeded, the autopsy room erupted in chaos. The procedure was halted, George's heart was started, and he was rushed to the hospital, where his recovery kept him for nine months. He was able to speak again within three days of his return, however, and what he said was almost as shocking to his friends and family as the fact that he was there to say it.

"The first thing I did was ask my wife to bring my friend whose child I had communicated with when I was out of body," he said. "I told them why the child was crying and asked them to have her X-rayed. They said it was impossible that I should even know about the child, much less that something was wrong." Of course, the X-rays proved him correct.

Even more unsettling to his wife was his ability to relate to her some of the thoughts she had while he was dead. "She watched me from a distance for a year before she could really accept all that had happened."

As remarkable, even miraculous, as George's near-death experience is—and it attracted a lot of local attention, much to the displeasure of the Soviet authorities—what's most inspiring is what George has done with his life ever since. The life that he was given back that day on the autopsy table, George has given to God.

"I wanted to be affiliated with the spiritual world or the church in any way possible," he told me, his eyes bright with the memory of the light and knowledge he had witnessed. "Prior to my near-death experience, I was a skeptical scientist. With the knowledge I touched in my experience, I understood there is a power greater than the human mind can comprehend."

He became an Eastern Orthodox priest, practiced "spiritual science" in a private research lab, and wrote and broadcast his message on Soviet radio and television, speaking regularly about early church history, theology, and the Bible. George's work touched the lives of countless people, offering a personal invitation to spirituality in a time and place where the church had at times been desecrated by government intervention. But George soon attracted the attention of the authorities, and once again his life was in danger. After an attack that left a bullet in his head, he told me, he went undercover until he and his family finally escaped. During a miraculous moment one night while he was in hiding, God once again spared him from certain assassination.

That night, face-to-face with the armed men whom he knew had come to kill him, George could do nothing but pray. "My eyes are looking right into their eyes," he told me, reliving the terror before me. "I know they are making eye contact with me. I don't know if I should just walk out and give myself up before they shoot me or let them come and forcibly drag me out of hiding.

"Tremendous, unending prayers are generating from deep within me, asking for the power of the universe to help me. Of course, I know we are looking at each other, and nothing can be done." But something was done, he told me. Though only five feet away, the men were not allowed to see him, and much to his astonishment, they simply walked away.

George remains astonished. "I still think about this," he assured me. "I am absolutely positive their eyes went through my eyes. This is an unanswered question for me, another unexplainable moment when my life was spared."

Freedom came soon after, and George and his family now live in Texas, where he is a Methodist minister, overjoyed at the opportunity to share his unique insight and spirit, free of any outside intervention. While some of the particulars of his description differed from my own, I could see that he spoke from the soul when he talked of his experience and the lessons it brought him.

George's experience shows us that God is all-powerful, and that God can take many forms. We do not all see a being of light, the Father and Savior I still think of every day. We do not all see Jesus. Some have told me they saw whatever spiritual leader is in their belief system, whoever brought them there. Others simply see a person they love; I've heard from some who were greeted by animals.

One of the most beautiful and touching experiences ever mentioned to me came from Laura, an artist who had died at the age of three, although she didn't understand that she had had a near-death experience until years later. At the time, she thought she had become an angel, and when she saw a lovely woman at her side, she thought that she was an angel, too. The angel told her to come with her, and she was led through a brilliant, peaceful light to the figure of "the most beautiful woman I have ever seen," Laura told me. "She had long flowing hair that was white and somehow golden. She was young-looking to me, but very wise, and she was surrounded by pink hues of light." The woman radiated love, much as the Heavenly Father did in my presence, and introduced herself to Laura as her mother—"my real mother, my heavenly mother," Laura said.

After a journey through a place of a beauty that Laura described in vivid detail, much like the garden that I visited, the heavenly mother told Laura she was to return to earth. "She told me that I would soon go back, but I would take with me gifts that would help me to live, grow, and be happy. She said I had important work to do on earth and that I would receive the help I needed. She told me that my love of color and beauty would always stay with me and that I would paint lovely pictures of color, joy, and light and be able to help other children to be happy, too."

Laura is a talented artist today. She is using her gift as her heavenly mother told her she would, even in her vivid description of the beauty she saw. And with his analytical mind and scientific background, George uses the gifts that he has to convey his experience. Sometimes he describes the source of the light and love and knowledge that filled him as God; at other times, it is "the infinite wisdom, or the infinite universal something, which we cannot grasp. It's impossible," he told me, "for us to comprehend our Creator."

But George could grasp the divine purpose that unites all of us, God's creations, as spiritual beings in material bodies: We here on earth are to grow spiritually as we pass through this world. "Time is necessary for earthly life to grow in every sense, for each person to connect themselves with eternity, and eternity with them, and to grasp the oneness of themselves with the spirit."

He saw that our purpose here is to participate in an awakening, which will happen, he says, when we "extend our spirituality so matter will be changed"—a time when we will actually feel our souls and materialize our thoughts. By doing so, he continues, we will create the kingdom of God on earth—unifying body and spirit, and feeling our unity with everything in the universe and with God.

"Part of Jesus the Christ's message was that the creation of the kingdom of God begins on earth, and each of us is a part of that. It is we who will create it. We are not only fallen angels, we are the angelic power within."

Our first step, he was shown, is to humble ourselves. "Being humble doesn't mean being weak; it means to be strong," he explained. "If you are humble, you are stronger than the strongest warrior of the world. We must lose ourselves to find ourselves. It is this new revelation, humbling ourselves . . . loving our enemies . . . that will connect us with infinity."

The transformation of the material into the spiritual is a cause for rejoicing, not for fear, he explained. By combining the material and the spiritual, "greater harmony will be created—harmony within soul, spirit, and body."

It gives me joy to hear the word of God spoken with as much love and conviction as I heard from George that night in Texas and have heard many times from him since. A friend, a healer, and a fellow pilgrim on this journey of awakening, George truly reaches people when he speaks of his miraculous experience and life transformation. When any man who returned to his body during an autopsy speaks of our need to create harmony between body, soul, and spirit, people are compelled to listen. When that man is a doctor, they listen even more closely. And when he is a doctor who has redirected his life toward the spirit, they listen closer still.

With his background and miraculous story, George

can reach people who can relate to his way of understanding and describing the divine. There is more than
one way of understanding it. I was told that others would
see as they needed to, that God gently leads us to the
truth as we will understand it. There really, truly is not a
way to explain the unexplainable.

When George and I talk alone, we speak very fluently.
We get excited. Since there is no language in the spirit
world that we are familiar with on earth, the knowledge
that is given there can only be given to the spirit. Then it
goes through decoding. George uses his way of decoding
what he experienced, I use mine, but the information is
the same. Whether you call it charity or love, the
message of God and awakening is the same.

We never know God's exact plan for the people in our
lives. Still I can't help thinking that George's unique
ability to speak the word of God must be part of why he
was twice miraculously rescued to continue his work
here when others tried to stop him. I was shown the
angels hovering above the earth, cheering us on, directed and protected by their love. I was taught of
our ability to call down thousands of angels to our aid
when we ask in faith, and I know they helped George
defy his earthly pursuers and continue on his path to
help us all.

The hand of God is clear in George's dedication to his
message. I was shown the universal law of giving and
receiving: When you receive love or knowledge, you pass

it on, and thereby leave yourself to receive again. If you hold on to it, you don't leave room to receive; you don't need it, because you don't use it. Use what you have, and you'll receive more. This is true for all of us. Knowledge without revelation is dead; knowledge held on to goes nowhere and helps no one. But the knowledge that we reveal to others takes on a life of its own, and allows us to receive more knowledge to share.

This is one reason why I give so freely of the knowledge I have received. I know I am meant to do so. And as a result, I have the opportunity to receive more, to be the student as well as the teacher. So it was with George, whose experience I would never have heard if I hadn't shared my own.

I thank God that there are miracles like George, who can share his own awakening to remind us all of the awesome power of our creator. His message of love and faith and hope is available to anyone who wants to take it; like the talent that young Laura was given by her heavenly mother, it is a gift to be shared. But we must accept the power of God if we want to enjoy the effects of it in our lives. And once we accept it, like George, we must pass on to others our knowledge of its power. The responsibility is ours.

The Awakening Heart

While I was in the spirit world, many things that were to come in the years ahead were revealed to me. More have been revealed in my journeys here on earth. Sometimes I am given the dates on which these events will happen, but their timing has seemed less important than the events themselves. One very important event that I have been shown, whose timing is *now*, is the spiritual awakening of some of God's ancient people. It is happening today, and it is part of God's plan for all of us.

These people are sanctioned by God, and he directs and guides their lives. Their ancient knowledge and understanding of the Creator, our Father, was preserved and kept pure in their cells. Their missions are those of teachers; they are shepherds who by their love will guide others to the path of God. All of these unique people were hand-picked by him, and I was shown thousands of these valiant souls as they chose to step forward, forsaking tradition by following their hearts. Because we have choice in heaven as well as on earth, we are considered volunteers when we answer God's call, because we *choose* to listen and accept his will. Many souls volunteered to do this service before coming to earth. Others were called to the work as their hearts later opened to God, having endured trials that made them open vessels to be used by him.

As this was shown to me, I was aware that a majority of those selected chose to come to earth as Native Americans. I was told that their knowledge of the ancient ways and their understanding of the Creator were pure. Many others were placed in positions of strength where they would open doors that would otherwise be closed to the Native Americans. In heaven we are not members of any race, but we choose to come to earth in different races so that the differences may help us in our spiritual development.

Others in the spirit world selected some of the lowest positions on earth to learn the compassion that would help them to be of greater service in the awakening. As they prepared for their callings, they suffered many hardships, because through hardship they could strengthen themselves and overcome their weaknesses. I watched many struggle as they shed the deceptions of the world, their hearts awakening to God's call. Angels stood closely by, watching. As heavenly beings, these angels had chosen to help in the awakening by being guardians to those who came to earth. The angels rejoiced as they watched the progress of the chosen spirits on earth, encouraging them by letting them know they were not alone. The angels sang songs that created energy, and that energy was directed to those in their care. They also sang songs of praise to our Heavenly Father.

Many spiritual beings had prepared for eternities to do their part in God's plan. They chose this work because of their level of development and knowledge. Our relationship to God and his plan was placed in our spiritual memory and was passed along through generations of cellular memory, all preserved until *its* time. The awakening of those cells recalls memories stored eons ago. That restored information includes memory from *all* senses, even of taste, touch, and smell. Those "called" will know that they have been, because of the awakening of all their senses, and they will be compelled by them.

The awakening of my cells began slowly, and I didn't understand it at first. In the years after my return to earth, I would at times experience a change in my emotions, as distant memories were recalled by my senses. I could remember villages as though I had lived in them, food that I still craved, and clothing that I could smell as though I were wearing it now, and many other things of a physical nature. Spiritual memories also surfaced as I recalled information that was given to me to be remembered in its time. But full understanding of my awakening eluded me for many years. Flashes of the knowledge I had been given would come to me, only to disappear as I attempted to comprehend. This knowledge often came to me at the most unusual times and in the most unusual ways . . . as a sound, a movement, a dream, a vision, or a craving for food that I did not recall ever experiencing. A movie about the Native Americans and their plight would bring tears to my eyes and emotions that filled my spirit with a passion that would not be quieted or dismissed. All of this and more began the awakening in me.

As I discovered that Native American spirituality was among the veins of knowledge I was increasingly able to tap, I became more receptive to the tide of understanding that began to rise within me. God showed me what I needed to know. I understood that the concepts of Native American belief were going to be of great importance to us all—not just sweat lodges and sun dances as the expressions of knowledge, but the Native Americans' abiding love and respect for the presence of God in everything. I saw the power of understanding that God is the creator of all things, who gives freely to us all. I saw the value of their humble attitude toward God, their practice of keeping ego and man-made religion out of their relationship with God. I saw the knowledge that lay in the Native American respect for family, self-sacrifice, and the spirit of God in nature. And I saw that it all goes back to love. We are like salmon swimming upstream, trying to get back to it, driven by the same natural instinct to get to love, because with love comes the honor and respect that the Native Americans teach. While other, newer belief systems became intertwined through the years with the pure ways of the old, the ancient ways were preserved by God in these people, to be awakened in many whom he has chosen.

Further revelations took me some time to understand. I saw that Satan's desire to govern the earth and its people was one of the reasons for this awakening call. The *Grandmothers* of the world, I saw, will foil Satan's plan to undermine the nurturing power of women and destroy the family. They will triumph not by force but by their wisdom, showing their strength in government and in the home, insisting that society act out of concern and care and not because of laws or legislation. They will demand the return of the parenting role to the parents and the support of the community to the family. They will take an active role by teaching the young the *respect* and *love* for all things that is best taught and learned in the home. While the woman's role is one of spirituality and wisdom, the role of men will again become one of support and strength, returning to their natural role as protector of the family. I marveled at what was shown to me, these simple truths that have been overlooked.

In my desire to continue to serve God and my people, I began to see my role unveil itself. Still not understanding all that I saw, I prayed for further enlightenment and knowledge of his wisdom and the patience to wait as my spirit was prepared to do his will. More was given to me and continues to come. When it is in its time, I pray to be used as he needs me.

I have been led to many other people who, like myself, are in a state of awakening. Each person is in the right place and at the right level, where their work will be most effective. Teachers were sent to me by the spirit, and they brought me messages of truth and then told me of places where I could find more. I began to understand some valuable information that made some of the knowledge that I received clearer to me. I have learned that to the Native Americans *grandmother* means "woman of wisdom," whether she is actually a biological grandmother or not. The earth, too, is recognized as mother earth or grandmother.

The spiritual beliefs of the Native Americans and their relationship with God are of a personal nature, like that of a child to the parent. God is known as Wakan-Tanka to the Lakota—the the father, the grandfather of us all, or the wisest, Holiest One, our Creator. He gives us our divine spirit, which is our life source, then when planted into grandmother/mother earth, it becomes the earthly source, its power. By grandmother, mother earth, we are nurtured. We carry within us the power of pure knowledge that was placed in our souls as seed. As it grows within our hearts, we are awakened to God. Our bodies are wakan (holy), because they are the temples of Wakan-Tanka and he dwells there. From our thoughts, seeds are produced. By the use of our tongue, our word, we plant them. By our deeds, we nurture them. These are the simple truths etched into the beliefs of a not-so-forgotten people of God, held there for generations for a purpose, now called to be awakened, by you, by me.

As my awakening heart recalls memories of a distant past, the world of my fathers, I've come to know that my present journey is just beginning and that there are many strange and wonderful things yet to experience, and yet to share.

The Place Where Our Spirit Dwells

*I*n each of us, I have learned, there is a place where our spirit dwells. We are born to this earth with our soul, the pure part of us we bring to earth from the spirit world. As we develop, we lose some contact with that spiritual part, our divine self, in a process of forgetting that is necessary for our development. But we can lose too much, and when we have lost all awareness of our divinity, we become spiritually disconnected and depressed. To feel whole again, each of us can and must reconnect with our spiritual self; since we are all at various levels of spirituality, each of us reaches this understanding in his or her own unique way.

My spiritual understanding was transformed when I

had my near-death experience. It was then that I was first brought in contact with my higher self and acknowledged the love of God. I came to recognize that my soul, my spirit, is connected with the flesh for only the short period of time that we are here on earth. The flesh and the spirit can work in unison, or they can struggle in conflict. I have come to see how often they are in conflict in my own life—those periods when the transitory desires of the flesh are being satisfied at the expense of my spirit. It is at those times that I am the most confused and unhappy, and I do not feel complete or serene.

I have learned that seeking a balance between body and spirit is essential for mortal well-being, as well as for mental and physical health. When I am in this balanced state, my spirit is no longer at the mercy of my body. I was taught in the spirit world that the spirit can control the flesh, raising temporal desires to a higher, more spiritual level, and I have seen this to be true in my own life. It is when we achieve that kind of balance that we function most creatively, spiritually and naturally, while we are here on earth.

When I begin to feel the separation or lack of balance between flesh and spirit, I have learned to enter a quiet place within me and reflect on my spiritual needs. Everyone has a different way of reaching that quiet place; some people get in touch with the inner self by using the assistance of incense, music, rituals, or other aids. There is no single, correct way to do so. What works best for me is simply to allow myself to become very still, something I can do anywhere, at any time. Then I invite God's presence to enter. As I contemplate that unseen, spiritual part of me, I feel it expand to become the greater part, filled to overflowing with his love. When my ego tries to dominate, I have learned to release myself and allow the spirit to prevail. Then I am calm again. I return to a deep sense of peace and knowing that can be felt only when my spirit is in tune with God and I can sense his presence within me.

For me to be able to comprehend this, I first needed to understand some greater truths. The most profound of these is the awareness that God exists—not just as an idea but as a being, a Spiritual Father—and that I am his creation. I have come to know that the many religious faiths have different ways of experiencing and expressing God. Each person becomes aware of a sense of God's presence and the spirit's divinity in his or her own way; where I once resisted this concept, I can now accept it. I can also see now that caring for the spirit is something that cannot be done just through rituals. Rituals can be helpful, but when we become too deeply involved with them, we tend to focus on the rituals and not upon the spirit.

I always wanted to be in tune with my spirit, but I saw that this was a process that I had to develop until it became as natural to me as breathing. Through prayer and stillness, I began to develop the ability to be naturally in touch with my spirit. In my own life, an important part of this process was expanding my awareness of the many concepts of love. This openness encompassed not only the love I have for other people, but the love of everything I see and the appreciation for all the beauty around me.

Gratitude, I have learned, keeps me in tune with my love and appreciation of the abundance of God in my life. When I awake in the morning, I thank God for each new day. I thank him for everything that I have, materially and spiritually, even the opportunity to grow from experiences that may not seem so positive but which I know are sent to me with divine purpose. I ask him to allow me to expand beyond my narrow-mindedness and self-centeredness, so that I can see the good that comes from everything.

My spirit is constantly being challenged, but as I grow and become stronger, my spirit becomes stronger, too. As I grow, my challenges also become greater, but I know they will never be so great that I cannot handle them. We may see people facing one challenge on top of another and wonder whether they can take one more thing. Their growth is enhanced by their willingness to take what appear to be negative events and turn them into something very positive. These individuals continue to grow and expand at a tremendous rate, unlike others whose lives just drift along. We can learn from them, and we can grow by sharing our love in support of them.

Our relationships with other people can present powerful windows of opportunity to help us grow in spiritual understanding, but we must be open to seeing those opportunities. Time and again I have seen that the people we need will come into our lives at the right time. This starts with our families. As spirits, we all chose our earthly families because of the growth we can inspire and make possible in each other. We will also meet other people with whom we deeply connect, spiritual sisters and brothers who touch us and help us to move on to even greater heights. There are spiritual lessons to be learned with people who seem not to be in tune with us at all and just pass through and out of our lives. Without our knowing it, they can act as bridges for us, enabling us to move from one level of awareness to another.

Clergy and churches can be a part of this network of spiritual sisters and brothers. Religion was not an important part of my life before my experience transformed my spiritual understanding. My search for God, to that point, was frustrated and inhibited by the religions in which I was raised. I have since learned a lot about religion. God is not about religion. Religion is a structure that should house our faith in God. Too often it is used to hurt other people in God's name. But I have also seen the good that religion and churches can bring us. We benefit from gathering in like-minded fellowship with others whose spiritual journeys resemble our own. We draw strength from each other and build strength by sharing the unconditional love of God with each other. And when we assemble in shared spiritual attunement and communicate together with God in prayer, the power of that prayer can be felt by all.

Counselors and therapists can also be guides for our spiritual journeys. Many people still see themselves as physical manifestations of the spiritual challenges of the families they were born into on this earth. We are, each of us, unique; we are born with what we need to grow spiritually, and that can include the family we choose on earth. Sometimes it is hard to see that we have within us the attributes we need to help ourselves; at those times, we may be able to develop a clearer vision of ourselves by leaning on someone else for a short period of time. I have always encouraged people who seek counseling for help; I've also encouraged them to move on if they feel that they are not progressing, because the *right* person, the one they need to be working with, *is* out there.

Through my own journeys I have learned that it often seems easier not to move on; even the muck and mire in which we are stuck often seems less fearful and challenging than the unknown path ahead. Some people use faith as a reason to remain stuck. They often say, "I have faith, so I'm waiting." But faith is not complacent: faith is action. You don't have faith and then wait. When you have faith, you act upon it. Complacency actually shows a lack of faith.

I have developed my faith by placing God foremost in

my life. I have learned that I must maintain a large measure of peace within myself to do so; I must be in tune with the love that God placed in me. I know that God is love, and if I do not recognize that same love within me, I cannot express that love to others.

I seek out the spirit of God daily for my guidance. Over the years, I have used various touchstones to help me do this, and I found them genuinely helpful. But material touchstones often are not available to us, and there will come a time in each of our lives when they will not be available at all, when the only touchstone we will have will be our internal connection with God. Physical things are easily lost and can change with the passage of time. I know that some people have come to accept various touchstones as their physical connection to God, but anything material that is required for connection with God can interfere with our direct contact with him. I have found that touchstones can act as medicine when they are used temporarily, at a point in time when we need them to connect with God, but they are not meant to be relied on for prolonged use.

I go to be with God each day in my prayers, and that special place is available to me at any time I choose. More often than not, it is at the kitchen sink where I find myself alone. Time is precious, but the time spent in prayer during the first and last few minutes of the day can keep your spirit in tune with God. Prayers do not need to be elaborate; my own are often quite simple, like a conversation with a parent or a heartfelt "good morning" or "good night" expressed with appreciation for God's love and generosity. Since taking the time to create the habit of prayer, I have felt closer to God in my thoughts, words, and deeds.

Our actions can also bring us closer to God. We are all at our best when we are most giving to others. When we are self-centered, love is difficult to find; when it is stilled, it is lost. Love is God's energy; it flows like electricity or like a current. When you release it and allow it to flow through you, it must flow out to others that you touch. It is a giving and a receiving. When we give love to someone, the love literally flows through us and we cannot help but feel it.

Each day, I put my life in God's hands and I say aloud, "Today I choose to serve God in every way that I can." As mortals, we do not know what our life's mission is. Only God knows, because only God's will can shape our purpose. We are powerless over God's will, but in our powerlessness lies our strength, for it is only through God that we derive true strength. He has given us free will, and he wants us to use it, but God's will can work through us far more powerfully than our own will can. We must remain open to God for his will to work through our spirit. Our spirit knows when we are on the right path. When we make a decision that we feel good about, we receive it as energy that propels us along a particular path. When we act in a way contrary to that path, we stumble and feel uncertain. Then it is time to sit down and reflect.

I was shown that we each have a purpose, and I have seen that many people try to find theirs. I do not know that we are all to know our purpose. We may sense that others have found their life purpose, when they seem to be doing what they were created to do, and we may yearn for that sense of purpose in our own lives. But I do not believe that it is important for us to know God's purpose for our lives. He knows, so we don't have to; we are only here to serve. It is less important that we know our purpose than that we serve it well. And he gives us what we need to do that. Our passion is the energy through which we serve our purpose. When we serve our purpose, we feel our passion. By following our passion, we will tap into the energy God gives us to serve our purpose.

I do not feel that I know my life's purpose. But I try to serve it by following my passion in each day. It is my desire that God's will be expressed in me for whatever reason. I believe that rather than trying to find out what my mission is, it might be better to just live and let it happen. I prefer to keep myself positioned, or prepared, for whatever comes. I guess I don't want to miss out on anything.

God gives us signs of his will for us. Many of our experiences are orchestrated by his guardian angels.

They walk among us in greater numbers than we know, and they help provide us with the opportunities we need to progress in our spiritual growth. We can see their hand in daily life, though we may dismiss their deeds as coincidence. When we are in tune with God's will, we can see these coincidences as what they are: our windows into the divine.

God's plan for us is much grander than anything we can envision for ourselves. It encompasses all. So there is a particular reason to be where we are right now. It may be required for our individual growth and spiritual development. But we are here collectively as well, for each other; we are all participants in the awakening of the power and glory of God's love. Each of us is a piece of the entire puzzle of life; each of our puzzle pieces carries a part of that larger love we share. Since whatever each of us does ripples out to others, connecting us all, perhaps we serve best not by wondering why we are here but by just doing the best we can and leaving ourselves open to God. God is perfect in everything; he makes no mistakes. We are here to learn, and for us that includes making mistakes. Learning to love is our goal, and our connection with God will help us do that, if we let him.

God is approachable. He wants to hear from us; like our fathers on earth, he enjoys our one-on-one communication with him. God wants us to have things, both spiritual and material things. Nothing is wrong with asking for what you need. And you can be as specific as you need to be. God wants that. It is good to define what your needs are. How else will *you* know what you desire? Many of us don't, until we talk to God in prayer. God knows our needs before we pray about them, but he wants us to *know* and understand them.

The more knowledge I receive, and the more I understand my own spirituality and the spirituality of others, the more I realize that I need to obtain yet more knowledge. Once you become aware of something, it opens a door and draws you into its knowledge. You walk through that door, and then there are more doors you have to choose among. You select yet another door and walk through that one, then there are even more doors to choose among. It is a constant challenge and a constant process, each door leading to others each time.

I have learned always to look for the next door. Whenever we reach a point where we think we are fully developed spiritually, we must be careful; we could find that we are caught in a maze or dead-ended. There is no reason to want to stop developing spiritually, because the wonders through each door are more beautiful than the ones before. Our journeys are their own rewards. We must never cease to seek more truth and knowledge and the understanding of God and his love.

My Resolve to Continue

Christmas 1995 promised to be a joyous holiday season. All of the kids planned to celebrate it at our home with Joe, little Betty, and me, and we had invited other relatives to join us. When they arrived, everything felt wonderful and complete . . . until the telephone rang and we learned that Joe's brother, Tom, had suffered a massive heart attack. Already in the hospital, he was scheduled for an emergency quadruple heart bypass surgery. Although Tom was seventy-two years old, few people would have guessed that by his appearance; he is a strong man, healthy and full of life, but the prognosis sounded grim. When the surgery went better than expected, we all thanked God and asked him to give Tom the strength to recover. But something in Tom had changed . . . forever.

When I visited Tom at the hospital, he was sleeping and unaware that I was there. Joe and I stood with Tom's wife, Hallie, looking at his still body attached to the machines. It seemed strange to see him that way. Tom is not a quiet person; he is very animated and laughs a lot when he talks. Both Tom and Joe were born and raised in South Carolina, and Tom still has his southern accent. It is an absolute pleasure to hear him talk, especially when he is excited, and people enjoy being around him.

As I looked at him lying on the hospital bed, I couldn't help but think we might be saying good-bye to him soon. I thought about the many years I had known this man and the closeness we developed. But the main thought that kept coming to my mind was of the many times Tom and I sat across from each other and talked about God. I knew that Tom had not found God or ever even looked for him. The last time we had had a conversation about God, Tom assured me that God did not exist . . . for him, for me, or for anyone else! And he was *emphatic* about that.

Seeing Tom in such a vulnerable condition reminded me of my love for him. Even though much of our time together was spent in disagreement about God, I could not imagine not having him around. Tom was serious in his disbelief and anxious to tell me and everyone else that "there was no such person—ever!" As I stood there

I prayed that God would be forgiving of Tom's lack of knowledge. I remembered how I was loved unconditionally when I was greeted by Jesus. I was still seeking God, and I knew that God couldn't help but love Tom's sweet loving spirit, as all who knew him did. While I prayed, a sense of peace flowed through me, and I knew that God would bless him, even in his disbelief.

Joe visited Tom daily as his health improved, but I stayed home caring for a house full of sick people, as they endured bouts of chicken pox and flu, which plagued just about every visiting family member. Tom was released from the hospital a week after his surgery, and he immediately called Joe to ask him to bring me over for a private conversation . . . as soon as I could get there.

Joe and I drove to Tom's home that same day. It wasn't like Tom to be mysterious, but he did not mention to Joe any details of the private talk he was anxious to have with me. As soon as Tom and I were alone, tears began to roll down his cheeks. Speaking slowly and precisely in a voice that kept breaking, he began the conversation that I would never forget.

"I don't know exactly what to call it, Betty," he began, "but something happened to me like what you call your near-death experience. I thought about it, and for me, what happened was more like just talking to God."

"You talked to God?" I almost shouted. I couldn't believe what I was hearing! I had expected anything but this. Tom had never believed me when I told him about my experience.

"It was more like he talked to me," Tom answered, undisturbed by my surprise. Tears continued to run from his eyes, but he didn't bother to wipe them away. I handed him some tissue, but he just held it.

"Did you travel down a tunnel or see his light?" I asked him, impatient to know. "Tell me about it! I can't believe this, Tom, you of all people!" I was surprised . . . no, stunned! Happy! I began thanking God with all my heart, remembering my prayer at the hospital while Tom slept. I thought back to my visit in the spirit world and to the loving sense of humor that Jesus extended to me when I was unwilling to leave him. Knowing Tom's determination when he feels strongly about something, I wondered if Tom had put up a fight when he was sent back, and I thought of the gentle delight Jesus must have taken in Tom's willfulness.

"I don't remember going down a tunnel or seeing him," he answered, "but I know that he implanted information into me somehow, and he wants me to use it to help people."

Implanted information. How wonderful it was to hear someone who had just experienced God try to explain the way information is transferred. Tears began to sting my eyes as memories of twenty-two years ago filled my heart once again and brought back a yearning that I knew would always remain with me.

"When I felt his presence, I wanted to be with him," Tom continued, "but he said, 'Tom, you can't come home yet, and you will not come home until you get it right! You have to get it right!'" Tears ran down Tom's face and his body shook with emotion. I could feel his sorrow and I wanted to hold him, but his surgery was too recent. We sat next to each other, and we wept, crying about a loss that we both felt and for a God that neither of us ever dreamed we would know.

"I wanted to go home, like you said you did in your book," he continued. "I didn't believe you then, but now I know; it happened to me and I don't know why! I just can't figure it out. Why me? I haven't lived a Christian life; I didn't ever believe in him!"

"Why me?" Funny he should ask me that, I thought. I had just written about that question, and now it had been turned around.

"Why not you, Tom?" I responded defensively, then lightened the mood with a quick joke. "If I were God, I'd send you back!" He smiled but became serious again, more tears brimming in his eyes.

I could hardly believe we were having this talk. I wanted to jump up and give a high five or a YES! But I remembered the feelings Tom was going through and knew that he needed to express them. I thought about the rest of the family. They would *never* believe what I was hearing right now! *I* wasn't sure that I was hearing Tom correctly. It was almost more than I could bear to sit quietly and listen as my sparring partner and strongest opponent continued to share his similar experience and firm belief in God.

Tom was anxious to tell me more, and I could not wait to hear it. "Now all I have a desire to do is to tell people that he loves us, all of us, no one more than the others," he resumed. "All my life I have been a devil's advocate and argued against a belief in God with others. I was adamant. I believed that God did not exist. I was an atheist—anti-God, anti-Christ. I didn't teach my children about him either. Until I had this new feeling inside of me, I couldn't die, Betty. He won't let me until I tell everybody I know that he lives! He opened my heart and eyes and taught me that it isn't hard to be with him or to know him. All you have to do is open your heart. It is so simple and we made it difficult. I always stood my ground that there wasn't a God. Now I stand my ground with my new belief, and I'll not be budged. I've turned totally around—not by myself, but with his help.

"I was the worst candidate for what God wants done, but he wants me to do it. He told me I didn't have it right. He said that I have to make it right by telling others that I had it wrong before. He brought me to respect him and gave me a mandate to tell all who will listen. I can do it now; I have changed!

"He also said that he was tired of people wondering if he was a man or a woman. We shouldn't think of God as a man, or as a woman, but just as God. He told me that.

He said all the wars are man's will to use God for their purpose to control. All churches use God the same way. He doesn't like that. He also said material things are not the reason for our being here. I have never read the Bible in my entire life. But I was told that the Bible was put together by man. And only the writers know if it was inspired or not. Some of it was and some was not, he told me. It's a good book for beginners, but the most important thing is that you have to open up your heart and let God in."

My heart rejoiced each minute that I sat listening to Tom, and I remembered my own thoughts after my return. When I was "told" that life on this earth would not be long, I had first thought, *my* life. Now I was overjoyed to hear that this wonderful man had found God in plenty of time to share his experience with his children. I knew that Tom's extraordinary strength of conviction would be used by God in a way that only God understood.

"Tom, you remind me of another man, and I love to read about him. His name was Saul, renamed Paul, and you are *so* much like him."

"Saul? Who's he?" Tom answered. "Where did you meet him? Is he from the South?"

Oh, my heart, I thought, don't stop beating; I have to thrill to this innocence! I had forgotten that Tom had never read the Bible. He had never thought it to be a book that contained knowledge of God.

"When you first wrote *Embraced by the Light*," Tom continued, not wanting to change the subject to talk about another man, especially one not from the South, "I was upset and skeptical about it—both about what you said and what you wrote about there being a God. I didn't believe you, but I was pleased and happy about your accomplishments. But now . . ."

Tom's voice trailed off as he was again overcome with emotions that brought more tears. Caught up in my own thoughts and emotions that sought expression I could not give them, I waited until he could speak again.

"I'm open still," he said, and I knew he was telling me that he, too, was continuing to receive revelations after his return. "He keeps giving me messages that open my eyes more. I was brought to a point where he could talk to me, Betty. He had to catch me at my weakest moment, when I could be open enough to receive him. I was hardened before. He had to bring me to my knees, to the point of death, before I would listen to him. I have begun to read some of the Bible now, looking for something in regard to this, and I'm amazed that some of the things I learned from God are there. He had explained these things to me in some detail. I don't want to put down the Bible or the churches, but you will not get to him by using them alone. People must learn to pray and be one with him. We've gotten away from him, he told me, and he said that we must get back to him."

Reaching for another tissue finally to wipe his tears,

Tom looked deep into my eyes before continuing. "We have to do everything we can, Betty, to tell people about God from our perspective. I believe in Jesus. He is the son of God, just like we are all sons of God. But he is not the God, but the son, blessed and given the message of love to bring to the world. I knew that the spirit within us all sees the truth and knows that God can't lie to us. He *had* to bring me close to death in order to use me. Until I get it right, and share my experience with others, he told me, I can't come home.

"As you and I were sitting here talking, Betty, a wave came over me and I suddenly realized that I was given a message from God to tell you. You have been called by him to get the message across that he loves *everyone*. You are to keep doing this. You can't quit! He told me that." The look on Tom's face told me how seriously he meant what he was saying.

"It's Christmastime, Betty," he continued. "Do you know what this means? Can you believe it? I'm seventy-two years old, and just this year, December 1995, he gave me a present that has changed me forever. He gave me the gift of life!"

We had been alone together for some time before Joe walked in the door with Tom's wife, Hallie. I could see their looks of surprise when they saw Tom and me sitting at the kitchen table where we'd had so many debates . . . both of us now laughing and crying at the thought that we were sitting there together, praising God and wanting to tell the world about him.

When Joe and I drove away from Tom's home that day, I couldn't help but think about my life and its many changes since my experience with my Father in heaven, my God. I couldn't help but remember little Holly's message for me not to quit, so much like the one Tom had just shared with me. I thought of the mission Tom had been given and remembered that I, too, was told that I must fulfill my own before I can go home to God. I wondered what lay ahead.

I still ask myself the question, "Why me?" and I still don't have any answers. Maybe Joe came close to it that night as we drove home from Tom's. "I suppose if I were God, I would choose you and Tom," he said. "The one thing you have in common is that you are not easy to convince. But once you are convinced, you are both too stubborn and strong-headed to change your mind and back off. You just don't quit!"

I've thought about Tom's message of God's love and remembered the one given to me. The message from the Savior has never changed: "Above all else, we are to love one another." And for as long as I live, it is my resolve to share that message . . . and I won't quit!

If you would like to receive
Betty's newsletter, *Onjinjinkta,*
or if you would like to write to Betty, write:

Betty J. Eady
c/o *Onjinjinkta*
P.O. Box 25490
Seattle, WA 98125

Or visit Betty's Web site at:

http://www.pstbbs.com/beadie